D1523813

Helping Your
Child Survive
Divorce

Helping Your Child Survive Divorce

Mary Ann Shaw, Ed.D.

A Birch Lane Press Book
Published by Carol Publishing Group

A Birch Lane Press Book
Published by Carol Publishing Group
Birch Lane Press is a registered trademark of Carol Communications, Inc.

Editorial, sales and distribution, rights and permissions inquiries should be
addressed to Carol Publishing Group, 120 Enterprise Avenue, Secaucus, N.J.
07094

In Canada: Canadian Manda Group, One Atlantic Avenue, Suite 105, Toronto,
Ontario, M6K 3E7

Carol Publishing Group books may be purchased in bulk at special
discounts for sales promotion, fund-raising, or educational purposes. Special
editions can be created to specifications. For details, contact Special Sales
Department, Carol Publishing Group, 120 Enterprise Avenue, Secaucus, N.J.
07094.

Manufactured in the United States of America
10 9 8 7 6 5 4 3 2 1

Library of Congress Cataloging-in-Publication Data

Shaw, Mary Ann.
    Helping your child survive divorce / Mary Ann Shaw.
        p.   cm.
    "A Birch Lane Press book."
    ISBN 1-55972-406-4 (hc)
    1. Children of divorced parents.   2. Divorce—Psychological
aspects.   3. Parent and child.   I. Title.
HQ777.5.S53   1997
306.874—dc21   96-24275
                                                        CIP

To Bobby, Chris, Sue, Jill, David, Megan, Stephanie, Tiffany, Kathy, Brittany, Regen, Riley, John, Sara, Parker, Tommy, Steve, Katie, Jimmy, Kristin, Matt, Sam, Hunter, Collin, Andrew, Amy, and the one million children each year who, through no fault of their own, must go through their parents' divorce.

Contents

Contents

Foreword

My name is Jessica Rae Riley, formerly known as Jessica Morriss. When I was two years old, my parents were divorced. My mom fought for custody; my father wanted a piece of land. What became of me? Twelve years of hell. My mother tried everything to help me through the pain of such a drastic change, moving from love to a world full of hate and anger. My father, well, he did nothing. He didn't care. He had his land and a way to make my mother miserable—custody of me.

Today I can still remember some strange man pulling me away from my mother. This strange man I later came to know as my father. People ask me all the time how such a man received custody of me. It was a small town, a well-known family, and he knew all the right people.

My mother read every book, magazine article, anything she could get her hands on to help me adjust to my new way of life. My loving father? He gave me to my abusive stepmother to fend for myself.

On my fourteenth birthday, my father let me go live with my mother. I think he was scared that I would take him to court and expose years of abuse. Wonderful, I thought, now my father and I will be able to have a relationship. On my first trip to visit, I hoped to find a father who loved me and wanted me. What I found was a new girlfriend who didn't like me and made it hard for me. I was only there for two days before my father kicked me out of the house because his girlfriend asked him to. Wow, that was a strong blow to the heart.

On that day, July 14, 1991, I decided that a relationship with my father was never meant to be. I would just have to face it. Now every year on July 14, I celebrate my father kicking me out. Strange? No. Just a way to heal wounds.

Not long after this wonderful event, my mother introduced me to Dr. Shaw. At that time I was very apprehensive about going to a psychologist. I had been to several psychologists before. Some told me how wonderful my life was with my father. One of them actually called my mother to tell her that deep down I wanted my parents to get back together. Another one locked me in his room and made me cry by yelling at me and telling me that I was such a bad little girl.

It's understandable why I was so fearful of seeing another psychologist, but my mother insisted. When she dropped me off at Dr. Shaw's office my face was angry, and when she picked me up an hour later I was wearing the biggest grin she had ever seen. Dr. Shaw said that I had every right to feel betrayed by my father. From that day on, my relationship with Dr. Shaw grew. She became my confidante, my best friend. I could tell her everything, and she would help me find solutions.

She helped me deal with the anger and hatred I held for my father. I was working everything out. My life was looking positive. Then, two weeks before Christmas of 1994, I had a breakdown. Depression. All I did was sleep and cry. It was hard. All the memories that I had forgotten were pouring in. But Dr. Shaw knew what to do. She made me talk, think, and feel what I was experiencing. It was strange, but it worked.

I decided on my eighteenth birthday to change my name to Jessica Rae Riley, Riley being my mom's maiden name. I thought it would be the best step in helping me deal with, not forget, my past. Changing my name was the key to locking the door to that past, and I threw the key into a deep ocean never to be used again.

So far it has worked. I also decided, with Dr. Shaw's help, not to take my father to court in an attempt to ruin his life. Taking his abuse for so many years, it has been hard for me to trust other men. Anyone I have ever dated I doubted. I put them through hard tests of loyalty and trust. Until ten months ago, I did not trust any male except my grandfather. I have now found a terrific boyfriend who has shown me that there are good guys out there and not to be so quick to judge. He has helped me build my self esteem.

It has been five and a half years since my father kicked me out of the house. I'm a sophomore at Pepperdine University. My major—psychology. I decided that the world needs more exceptional psychologists like Dr. Shaw, and that through my experiences, I could help other children overcome the pain and agony of divorce and abusive parents. It has taken me five years to realize that the best revenge against my father is moving on with my life and making it better.

I hope that this book will help teach parents about divorce and the strong effect divorce has on children's lives. Dr. Shaw knows what she's talking about.

She saved me.

Acknowledgments

The stories on these pages are all true. They are the stories of my kids, the kids who come to my office each week to try to understand divorce and their parents and why life can sometimes be so hard. The kids gave me the idea for this book because they want their stories told. They want parents to understand what happens to children before, during, and after a divorce. I promised I'd try. So, kids, here it is.

Many of the illustrations used in this book came from work sessions incorporating the suggestions of Barry Bricklin, Ph.D., in his book *Perception of Relationships Test* (Furlong, Pa.: Village Publishing, 800-553-7678).

To protect the privacy of children and parents, names have been changed and situations altered throughout this book.

Helping Your Child Survive Divorce

1

Why Parents Need to See Divorce Through a Child's Eyes

SINCE I BEGAN working as a child psychologist more than a decade ago, I have watched divorce do more damage to children than any other single force. Over the years, the percentage of my clients who are affected by divorce has grown steadily. Now almost half of the children I see are from divorced families.

Even though adults know they shouldn't trash their estranged partners in front of their children, even though they know they shouldn't use their children to spy on their exes, even though they know they should get help when their own pain and resentment begin to overflow into their relationships with their children—too often, parents close their eyes and ears to what they know is the truth. Divorce classes for adults are readily available in churches, synagogues, and community centers, but too many adults aren't listening—to professionals or to their children.

The painful and frustrating situations that children are

3

placed in before, during, and after a divorce are a great source of worry for me. Nothing saddens me more than the helpless look in a ten-year-old's eyes when I ask her how things are going at home. Or the eleven-year-old who has to go into a psychiatric hospital for several weeks for depression because one parent is asking the child for help in reuniting with the other parent. Nothing wrenches my heart more than a five-year-old child who wants to be with his mom, but his mom has elected to be a single person and not a parent any longer. Nothing is more frightening than the child who leaves a note saying he wants to die because being in between his mom and dad is so stressful.

I volunteer my time at a place in Dallas called the Family Connection. It's a nonprofit organization that offers a service for split families having extreme problems and in need of supervised visitation because of abuse or alleged abuse, or who need a neutral zone to drop off kids for visitation because parents are so hostile to one another. On one visit there I saw a note taped to a doll still in the package. The note read: "The mother said that her child cannot take home any present her father gives her." Think about the message this mother's posture sends to her child. This parent, overwhelmed with anger, can no longer recognize her child's basic right to interact with both parents. Unfortunately, I find that this type of bitterness is not the exception.

Parents aren't listening to their children. They aren't thinking about the position they put their children in when divorce gets mean-spirited. Divorce, after all, is only for parents. Children will have two parents all of their lives, and often they'll have to learn the difficult task of how to love someone that someone they love hates.

Before, during, and after a divorce, parents are thinking about their own needs, and, too often, they fail to understand that their children are far more vulnerable to divorce than they are. Parents have a huge support group. They typically tell everybody about their divorce from the hairdresser to their good friends, neighbors, and coworkers. Usually, they'll find this circle of friends and acquaintances very supportive.

Kids don't have that built-in support system. Children often won't talk about their parents' divorce, even to their classmates and closest friends. They don't talk to teachers about it. Teachers usually find out through the grapevine of other parents.

It's natural in difficult divorces for parents' thoughts and actions to be dominated by hatred, extreme resentment, even obsession with inflicting pain on the ex-spouse. Their life is changing dramatically, sometimes not by their own choice, and, being psychologically in crisis, they have a number of self-serving reactions. But parents have to get a grip on themselves and bring the focus back to their children. That's what this book is all about: listening to and focusing on the child.

It is critical for children, especially children under six years old, to have healthy relationships with both parents. Disruptions in parent-child relationships during these important years can not only cause immediate developmental problems but also lead to a higher risk for anxiety, depression, and a variety of personality disorders.

Each year a million children are subjected to divorce. None of their experiences will be good ones. Even if parents do focus on their children, make rational decisions together in the best interest of their children, offer continued emotional and financial support, provide consistent messages of rules and discipline—in short, continue to be good parents even though they are divorced—children will still be heartbroken and feel torn between two households. "It's still hard going back and forth and dealing with all of this change," says eleven-year-old Jennifer, whose parents have been divorced for eight years and have a fairly amicable relationship. "I still wish we could all live together."

But when parents are hostile to one another, children often get lost in the mayhem, which puts their futures at risk. This issue is so far reaching in its effects on our society that it has attracted the attention of the U.S. Commission on Child and Family Welfare. In a report to the president and congress, the commission made specific recommendations to courts and state legislatures to help reduce the adversarial nature of divorce litigation in an attempt to save future generations of children of divorce. The commission's overall concern is that, without strong, healthy children, we won't continue to be a strong, healthy society. "Parenting Our Children: In the Best Interest of our Nation" is the commission's simple, yet often hard to realize, call to action for America.

Nearly 100 percent of the time, when I ask a child who is involved in a divorce how many children he or she is going to have, the answer is, "None." The reason, "I wouldn't put a child through this." That's a consistent answer for boys and girls of various ages. "I don't know if I'm going to get married," they'll say, "but I am definitely not going to have children."

If there's a "pre-divorce" shelf in the bookstore, that's where this book belongs. The ideal time to read about how divorce will affect your children is *before* the divorce gets started. Parents need to know what to expect and exactly how their actions along the way can hurt or help their children. If you are currently involved in a divorce, it's not too late to learn the valuable parenting techniques shared on these pages. Even if your divorce is behind you, but your children are having problems now, this book can open your eyes to the proper perspective.

It's important to understand that divorce doesn't have to be damaging to children—painful, yes, grief ridden, yes, but not damaging for the long term. Parents' actions have a profound effect on how divorce will change the child. In their groundbreaking research on divorce, Judith S. Wallerstein, Ph.D. and Sandra Blakeslee, authors of *Second Chances: Men, Women and Children a Decade After Divorce*, found that many of the children studied who grew up to be "compassionate, courageous, and competent people" were helped by good relationships with one or both parents, grandparents, stepparents, siblings, or mentors. Others succeeded in spite of the examples set by their parents.

But far more often, children of divorce grow up believing life would be much better if only mom and dad had stayed together. No matter how bad life was in the pre-divorce household, time after time kids tell me they want their parents back together again. Why? Because the split family isn't working, forcing them to daydream about the way things could have been—often into adulthood. Their perceptions of relationships are distorted and colored by their childhood experiences, caught as they are between contentious parents.

A split family that doesn't work can lead not only to problems with anxiety and depression but to difficulties involving loyalty and trust, discipline, manipulation, substance abuse—and can even lead to suicide. A University of Michigan study of one hundred forty-four children and adolescents whose parents had divorced, all of whom were patients at Children's Psychiatric Hospital, found that 63 percent suffered from anxiety, sadness, pronounced moodiness, phobias, and depression; 56 percent had poor grades or grades substantially below their ability or past performance; and 43 percent were acting out aggressively toward their parents. Another study, focusing exclusively on academic achievement, found that 30 percent of children studied continued to experience a marked lag in academic performance three years after their parents separated. Access to both parents appeared to be the most protective factor associated with better academic adjustment. The data also indicated that the more time a child spent with the noncustodial parent, the better the child adjusted to the divorce.

Over the years, I've seen it all, sometimes too late to make a difference, but usually in time to help parents and kids find a way to make a split family work. The foundation of this book is the basic parenting techniques that I share in therapy with my patients and their parents. When parents can listen to their children and, more importantly, hear and see themselves from their children's perspectives, many problems will be avoided or, at the very least, minimized. Divorce is traumatic for families, but by listening to the children in this book—and to your own children—and using the techniques and postures prescribed here, your children can survive divorce.

2

Logical Parenting—How to Answer the Tough Questions

THE BEST WAY TO HELP your children deal with divorce is to be better parents—not after you begin to see your child suffer from emotional problems or developmental delays, but starting now, from the beginning of the divorce process. In my practice, I try to teach parents common-sense, no-nonsense parenting skills that they can take with them from my office to their homes. What I call "logical parenting" is really just teaching parents how to distance themselves from their own emotional needs and put their children first.

This is not going to be easy. Parenting throughout and after a divorce is tough because everyone is at a different emotional level. No one is working in concert—certainly not the parents who are divorcing or the children whose world is crumbling. It's harder because everyone, including the children, is encountering different issues. Nothing is simple. Any request made by anyone in the family for anything is immediately suspect, fraught with underlying questions and emo-

9

tional baggage. Your job as a "logical parent" is to put your own needs aside for a moment and investigate. Peel back the layers of the onion and find out what your children need. Then try to give it to them.

The following are some of the most frequent questions and issues that come up during and after divorce, and logical-parenting solutions that help good parents be better parents.

"Will You and Mommy/Daddy Get Back Together Again?"

This is the most common wish of any child at any age. It will persist longer than the fantasy of Santa Claus. It will persist even if both parents are happily remarried. It will persist even if a child fits in well with a step family. It will often persist into adulthood.

Parents and stepparents have to understand that this is not a reflection on them. This is just the way your child is going to feel, and the only thing you can do is empathize. Reassure your child that you know how difficult this must be for him or her to have two families and such a complicated life, but that this is the way it is going to be.

By wishing this wish, your child is expressing her need for constancy of the family. Give her as much constancy as you can, and the wish won't dominate your child's thoughts. And realize, you may never be able to make this unrealistic desire go away.

"I Don't Want to Spend Friday and Saturday at Mom's/Dad's House. Just Saturday Is Fine With Me"

To a child, this may not be just a simple request but a test to see just how flexible you are willing to be with his schedule. In a sense, this child is asking, "Are you going to let me continue with my life?" Meanwhile, Mom or Dad is thinking, "Did my ex put you up to this?"

Every question is loaded during a divorce. As a logical parent, you have to unload the questions and the answers. Talk to your child. Weigh the request. Is it a test? Does he really want to spend the night with a friend? Maybe this is a friend you don't like too much? Do you usually say no when your child wants to spend the night with friends because you don't see him as often as you'd like?

Talk about it. Let your child know that you do want him to have a social life. But also emphasize that you want to spend time together and you are also trying to get used to this new routine. Let your child know that you want him to continue to have a good time with friends, so, this time, spending the night out is okay. Maybe next time the sleepover can be at your house.

It's hard for parents to be flexible with kids when they are no longer around them all of the time, but it is so important for your child to have a sense of normalcy. And being with friends, or sometimes just being at one home, is essential for normalcy.

The key is good communication. If you have good communication with your child, you will know when he asks you for a favor whether it's legitimate or whether there are ulterior motives behind it. The less you communicate with your child, the easier it is for him not to want to be with you. The trick to good communication is trying, gently and often, to discuss issues. In a divorce situation, it's going to be harder. The older your child gets without having good communication with you, the harder it's going to be to get to a place where you can talk and understand one another. So don't waste a minute. Start now.

"I Don't Have to Do That at Mom's/Dad's House. Why Do You Make Me Do It Here?"

If you and your ex can't agree on a set of consistent rules for your child to follow from house to house, then you risk hearing this question over and over again. The easiest way to explain to your children the inevitable differences that remain is by relating the situation to something they can understand. "You know that you have some things you do at school that you don't do at home. Well, this is the way this house runs best, and your mom's/dad's house runs best another way. I know it's hard for you to keep it straight, but I'll help by reminding you until you get used to it."

Take out the human element—"this is not something I am doing *to* you"—and put in the organizational element: "house rules." A kid is just naturally going to think, "You are being unfair to me." Like most of us, kids don't like change—especially when it applies directly to them. They want every-thing to be the way it used to be. It's important for you to empathize and then help them adjust to the change.

"I Don't Want to Go to My Mom's/Dad's House Every Week"

There can be many reasons why your child wants less visitation with your ex. A refusal to visit the other parent shouldn't be taken lightly because it's important for your child to have a relationship with both parents. Initially, I tell parents to treat these requests just as they would a request for an expensive present—something to work toward that won't materialize overnight. This will give you and your ex the time to do some detective work. Is it a valid request because the current visitation schedule is not working with your child's own busy schedule? Is your child a typical adolescent who is more interested in peers than in family? Is your child uncomfortable at the other parent's home? Does he feel like a stepchild because your ex has a "new" family?

If you give this request a lot of thought and you feel that the best thing for your child is to change the visitation schedule, then try to do that. If you involved your ex in the detective work, he or she will be more willing to work for a solution that benefits your child. Even if you have to go to mediation or back to court to get it done, it's worth it if it will make your child more comfortable.

Too often visitation schedules are set by nonfamily members who know very little about your child and often don't understand developmental stages of growth. Your child may not be ready for the schedule set out by the court. The court may have looked only at what's convenient or fair to the parents—not at what works best for the child. So, if it's not working, it's your job as parents to find something that works better.

"How Can I Go to Camp in the Summer When I Have to Go Live at My Mom's/Dad's?"

There is nothing more burdensome to a child than to experience the guilt placed on her by a parent. If that parent spends the school year pumping up "everything we are going to do when you're with me this summer," it makes it extremely difficult for a child to ask to go to camp. This is the type of emotional scenario that makes kids of divorce give up on things—wishes, dreams, and aspirations. It starts with something as simple as wanting to go to camp and seeing that as an impossible request. Soon, anything the child wants is out of reach.

Parents do this to children when they put their own needs

first. Parents think, "I have this child for a limited amount of time, and I have to make sure she is loyal to me and involved with me." But being with you for six solid weeks in the summer is not going to make your relationship indelible. Giving your child what she needs, on the other hand, can work wonders.

I encourage parents to look not at what they need but at what their child needs. There are a lot of children, especially only children, who need the camp experience to become independent. Kids of divorce may need to go to camp even more because it's important for them to break from what's going on between you and your ex. Or you may be smothering them out of your own guilt and preventing them from growing into independence. Divorced parents—often because they have fought so hard for "possession" of their children—forget what I consider to be the most important rule of logical parenting: you raise your kids to be independent and to leave home whole and healthy.

"At Mom's/Dad's House I Can Wear Makeup, Why Can't I Wear It Here?"

Adolescence is all about testing values, and if a divorced child's two homes are diametrically opposed on child rearing issues, it really can make a child feel schizophrenic. If your child wants to wear makeup, and if she can wear it at your ex's house, you are only going to push her into deceiving you by persisting to deny it.

When it comes to making rules about dress and makeup, I encourage parents to go to their child's school. Walk the halls, go into the classroom, attend assembly, go to the football and basketball games. Judge for yourself what the norm is. Parents need to encourage their children's desires to fit in. These desires are healthy. Wanting your child to look as though she stepped off of the set of *Little House on the Prairie* is probably not going to be practical in today's world. If you are so shocked by what's going on in your child's school, then maybe you and your ex need to talk about sending your child to a different school. Otherwise, get comfortable with the norm and with your child wanting to be part of the social life around her.

"Why Do I Have to Go to Bed Now? We Can Stay Up Until Ten O'clock at Mommy's/Daddy's"

One of the most often cited reasons for divorce is that parents disagreed on how to raise the children. If that was something that caused frequent arguments before you were divorced, don't expect the problem to be miraculously solved just because you now live in two different houses. On the contrary, it will probably get worse. However, with this question and a thousand others like it, you have to realize that certain things are out of your control and learn to live with them.

I tell the parents of the children in my care, who argue over every little issue, to pick their battles. It's probably best to limit those battles to only the most important topics—things like school or religious education—rather than issues that fall into the category of house rules. If your child is doing poorly in school because he or she isn't getting homework done or enough sleep at your ex's house, that's a battle worth fighting.

Try not to get caught up in a game of control with your ex. Hang on, keep quiet, and almost everything that falls into the less important categories will work out in the end.

"I Want to Go Live at Mommy's/Daddy's"

Expect to hear this plea many times as your child grows up. Your job is to discern when it is a threat, used in an argument to try to get you to give in to something, and when it is truly a need that you should try to fulfill. Regardless, your posture should be the same. Your answer is, "Well, that's between you and your mom/dad. I tell you what, tomorrow we'll call him/her and set up a time, and you can talk about it. You two let me know what you decide."

If your child was just trying to win an argument, that should diffuse it. If your child really is ready to go live with his other parent—which will often happen around puberty— this will begin the process.

I usually suggest that parents don't make these switches quickly. Set a deadline about a month ahead, which will let your child really ponder the move. And make sure everyone agrees that the new residence will be in effect for six months or a year before you all sit down together and discuss it again to make sure it is working.

Remember, your divorce isn't over for your children when you sign the final papers. You and your ex will be parenting together for the rest of your child's life.

3

The Beginning of the End—
"My Mommy and Daddy Can't Get Along"

THE DAMAGE FROM DIVORCE can start long before the legal proceedings begin. While you may think you're hiding the anger and arguments from your children, you're probably kidding yourself. Bet instead that your children are in tune to the moods and the temperature of your relationship with your spouse. Perhaps even more in tune than you are. Very young children may not have a large speaking vocabulary or be able to decipher those choice words you spell out in front of them, but they do know how to read body language remarkably well. After all, they've been doing it since before they were born.

Illustration 1: Girl, age 7, "They think I can't hear them when I'm in bed or watching TV."
I asked this child to draw her family doing something. What I got was the only thing many children of divorce see their families doing together—arguing.

17

Illustration 1

It's widely known and well documented that parental discord is stressful and upsetting to children and can result in disciplinary problems at school and at home, poor grades, substance abuse, or violent acting out. Boys in particular have problems when their parents fight. One study of a hundred families, approximately half with a daughter and half with a son, found that boys from families with fighting parents reacted by showing "more immature social relations, poorer impulse control and less effective ability to cope independently" than boys from families with little arguing or than girls from either tranquil or discordant families.[1]

Worried, anxious, afraid, sad—these are the feelings children have when their parents fight. And no matter what the source of the argument is, children will tend to think they alone are to blame.

"I Felt Lost and Panicked"

Rosie was ten years old when her parents' arguments escalated toward divorce. She says when she heard them arguing, she felt lost and panicked. A bright girl, she was old enough to understand exactly what was going on and to predict the worst: divorce. She imagined her whole world crumbling—and then she saw it start to happen. Though Rosie's situation was bad, she says that while she was unhappy when her parents argued, she dreaded divorce even more. Similar to abused women, she would rather have kept her family intact, as unhealthy as it was, than to give it up and live as a split family.

"I Never Thought *My* Parents Would Get a Divorce"

On the opposite end of the spectrum, Judd is an eight-year-old boy whose parents made a pact never to argue in front of their children. They were better than most at hiding their discord, and Judd and his siblings were traumatized when their father walked out. Though the parents knew they were separating, the children were in shock, hurt, and full of questions.

So what's the correct posture to take with your children? Certainly arguing in front of them about any adult matter—infidelity, finances, decisions over school or health care—should be avoided. Those discussions, if they are going to be heated, are best handled behind closed doors, after bedtime, or out of the house in neutral territory. But at the same time, don't leave your children completely clueless. Translate your situation with your spouse into something they will understand, "You know how you feel when you are arguing with your friends. Well Daddy (or Mommy) and I are having trouble agreeing right now."

At this pre-divorce stage, your ability to compromise will often leave you. As a result there are arguments and no immediate resolutions. In this state of mind, parents have a hard time determining how much their children should know and how much they shouldn't know about what's going on in the marriage. Here's a good general rule: they don't need to know *why* you are having arguments but only that you are having a difficult time agreeing. Always end this discussion with positive reinforcement that the arguing is about adult things—not about them—and that you and your spouse will always agree on one thing: loving them.

"I Know This Is All My Fault"

If you don't sit down with your children and discuss your problems and their fears, expect them to assume that they are the problem. This is a universal assumption among children of all ages. Often kids will reinforce this assumption with their own bad behavior. They are thinking, "If I'm really bad, then maybe they'll worry about me and leave each other alone." They are acting up in order to force you and your spouse to forget about your own problems and focus on them.

The following are some special concerns that relate particularly to certain age groups:

Infants and Toddlers

Many parents who are not getting love and affection from their spouse will hold or cuddle their children when they are upset. After a big fight, they'll go in their children's room, get them out of the crib, and hold and rock them. When you are upset, your infant or toddler will pick up the tension. He or she won't feel warm and nurtured because Mom or Dad is not in a warm and nurturing mode but in a needy mode. It's very common for a parent to turn to physical contact with his or her child because there is none with the spouse. But this reaction to the early stages of the marital breakup is confusing for a child who expects to be the protected not the protector.

Sometimes during this final stage of a marriage, a mom will start sleeping with her infant or toddler as a way to avoid being in the same bed with her husband. This, too, should be strictly avoided because it gives a regressive, needy message to the child.

"Will You Always Be My Daddy?"

As the end of the marriage and the beginning of the divorce near, use the fewest number of words possible to tell your toddler what is happening. Both parents should do this together. Breaking the news could go something like, "Mommy and Daddy are not happy. We think it's a good idea for me to move to another house. I won't be here when you go to bed, but I'll call you on the phone and you can call me."

Give the child phone numbers and a photograph of the parent who is moving out. For children this young, keep the connection on a regular daily basis if at all possible. Start spending time with the child separately—immediately. Ideally this has been well established even while the family was together. Try taking your child to breakfast, or stop by for a prearranged walk around the block or to the park. Brief but regular contact will help your child feel connected to both parents, which should be a constant goal throughout and after the divorce.

Ages Six to Twelve

At this age, with peer influence growing stronger, children may choose to "check out" of their quarreling family and, out of confusion, turn to a friend's family for love and support. While studies have indicated that peer support can be a great source of strength for children now and throughout the divorce process, it's still best for parents to try to minimize confusion and emphasize that they are still the primary support system for their children.

"I'll Take Care of You Now, Mommy"

There is a great tendency for mothers to tell boys of this age group, "You are the man of the house, now." While it's common for a male child of this age to want to assume that role and soothe a hurt parent's feelings, this can be very damaging. Be careful when you do your sobbing. Do it with your friends and not your children. If your children know you've been crying, make it clear that they're not the cause. Resist the temptation to put blame on your spouse.

As the divorce progresses, acknowledge that, at times, everyone is going to feel sad about the divorce. Introduce the concept of parents having "blue time." When you feel blue, you need some time to yourself. Go in your room or on a walk or to a movie to do your brooding. Then get over it. Make sure your children know they can always come and talk to you about their own blue feelings and that your blue feelings don't have anything to do with them.

Again, as with children in the younger age group, identify for your six to twelve year olds that you and your spouse are having trouble being kind to one another and agreeing. Talk about the future only in the short term, "I don't know what's going to happen. We are talking to see what's best for ourselves and for you." Identify each step for your child four or five days ahead of time. "Being in the same house is not helping our feelings get better, so we have decided that Dad (or Mom) will move somewhere else." The worst thing to do is have one parent pack and leave the house when the child is not at home. That is true rejection, and it causes you to have to go into far more detail and explanation than if you had involved your child step by step.

If a child this age overhears your arguments, apologize. "I'm sorry that you heard us arguing about our problems. You really shouldn't have had to hear that. These are grownup problems and have nothing to do with our feelings about you and how we love you or care about you. We'll try our best to keep that from happening again."

Children of this age will have some questions, but keep your answers general. If the answer to their question of what's going to happen is, "I don't know," that's okay. If the answer is, "We are going to go to counseling, but we don't know if it's going to work," that's okay, too. Don't try to paint a rosy picture. Kids are not dumb. Just briefly communicate the facts.

It can be helpful to children of this age for you to let their teacher know, privately, that divorce could be imminent. This will help your child's teacher understand behavioral changes. Stay in touch, and the teacher will be able to keep you abreast of developing problems.

Teenagers

Teenagers are naturally self-centered. Their main concern is going to be, "How is this going to affect me?" "Am I going to change schools?" "Can I still go to the football game Friday night?" Don't expect much patience and understanding. A teenager's attitude is going to be, "My parents are dumb and stupid for getting a divorce." Their ability to understand is limited because of the stage of life they're in. However, if yours has been a very violent and uncomfortable home, your teenagers will probably push you toward divorce—not because they are worried about you but because they figure life will be better for them afterward.

"Why Are You Doing This to Me?"

By this age, in most cases, there is really no need to assure your child that the divorce is not their fault. They will be concerned about the consequences for themselves. Expect anger. From their perspective, you are "doing this to them" just at the moment when they are beginning their lives. What does this mean to them? Can she still buy that new prom dress? Are they still going to be able to go to college? Will their friends find out?

There is a tendency for teenagers of divorcing parents to be cynical and depressed. It is important for every parent to understand that divorce is a loss for a child of any age. Your child will go through the same emotional stages, from anger to acceptance, that you experience—probably not at the same time. So don't try to force your own steps of this process on your teenager. Your teenager will have feelings you won't have. He or she may be embarrassed. They may not want to tell their friends. They may begin to gravitate to friends from split families. They may be concerned that parents of friends from whole families won't let their kids associate with them anymore.

Respect your teenager's growing independence and need for privacy. Don't jump the gun and go to school to run interference for him or her, exposing the impending divorce situation to a teacher or counselor. Offer constancy and support to your teenager. I find these to be magic words for children of all ages, "You'll get through this. Whatever you need, let me know, and I will try to get it done." Let your children know you are there to help when they ask no matter what is going on between you and your spouse.

Telling your teenager not to be angry or depressed makes about as much sense as a child telling a parent not to get divorced. Instead, acknowledge their anger and let them know you understand they're mad. When they say, "Life sucks," you say, "Yeah, it does right now, but it's going to get better." Then make sure it does get better.

4

Separation—"My Mommy and Daddy Aren't Going to Live Together Anymore"

TELLING YOUR KIDS that one of you is going to move out is one of the hardest things you will ever have to do as a parent. It's even more difficult than talking to them about sex. You are hurting, and you know this news is going to hurt them. Still, it's important to focus on your children and put your arguments and personal feelings aside. This exercise—breaking the news—is good practice for what's to come in your divorce.

The most mature way to handle the situation, and by far the best for your children, is for both parents to sit down and explain that, in spite of trying to get along, you have both reached the decision that living in the same house isn't working. Therefore, it's best for Mommy (or Daddy) to move out for a while. The same rules for sharing information discussed in the preceding chapter apply here. Just the facts, please. And grown-up reasons for the separation should be left private, just between the two of you, and not shared with your children.

It's important to reiterate that the conflict between you has nothing to do with your children. You don't have to go into great detail, but just make sure your children hear this message, "Our separation has nothing to do with you." Of course your children's response will probably be, "It has *everything* to do with us." They're right to the extent that your decision to separate affects them deeply. So be more specific if necessary, saying, "If we have ever argued about your activities or anything you were doing, those arguments don't have anything to do with this."

Keep in mind that even young children will remember this moment for the rest of their lives. Pick the time and place for this family meeting wisely according to the temperament of your child. Privacy is important. Stay calm and don't become overly emotional. Your child needs to believe that you think this is the best and only course to take. If you get upset, he'll be even more upset and confused. Make sure that he understands he will be taken care of—whether the family is living in the same household or not.

Now twelve years old, Sara can vividly recall the night eight years ago when her father told her he was leaving. It was her bedtime, and her dad came in, sat down beside her, and told her he was going to move out of the house. She remembers crying and then, "I made him sing me three songs and kiss me sixty times." The fact that her mother wasn't there was a source of confusion for Sara and a hint of the extreme discord between her parents that would reveal itself as the divorce progressed.

"Did Mommy make Daddy leave?" or "Did Daddy leave us behind?" are common questions for children whose parents fail to communicate that their decision to separate was mutual. Your goal is to leave your child thinking that you made this decision together and that you both think it's best. If you don't do this, if your child wakes up one morning and mommy or daddy is gone, he may very well fear that the parent who remains at home could just go away, too.

This fear explains why some children refuse to go to school, or once there, "get sick" in order to come home. Other children become fearful of leaving home at all and refuse to spend the night with friends or play at friends' houses. Their logic is, "If I am with her at home, nothing bad will happen."

"What If I Need You?"

If you are the one leaving, answer this question before it's asked. "If you need me, I'll be here. Just because I don't live in the house with you doesn't mean I won't be available to you." Clue your child in to what your next few days are going to be like. "I found a place to live, and I'll be getting settled there. Here's the phone number. I'm going to take you over there so we can get your new room together, too." Don't tell your child you want them to help you get settled. You don't want to put her in the position of feeling like she is encouraging the separation or in the role of caretaker.

Do everything you can to be accessible. Set up a regular time to talk on the phone, such as before bed or when your child comes home from school. Be consistent so that this contact becomes routine for you and her. Get a pager so that your child can reach you any time. Our society is such that out of sight is often out of mind. So, especially for the younger child, make sure she has a picture of you in her room.

"How Many Sleeps Until I See You?"

Younger children, especially toddlers younger than twenty-four months, have difficulty understanding that you are going to come back when you are gone. Even children ages two to six can have trouble understanding "tomorrow." Your three- or four-year-old toddler may grasp days by counting the number of "sleeps." But the concept of time, as in "I'll see you next weekend," is difficult for children to grasp until about age seven, when time is introduced in school.

For this reason, the younger the child, the more constant the contact needs to be with both parents. This is difficult on parents, especially in this early stage of separation when emotions are so volatile. However, it is the most critical period for children. Some routine needs to be set up so that the parent who has moved out can keep daily contact with a young child. Children under three have less tolerance for separation. Even a daily phone call to your child while he or she holds a big picture of mommy or daddy will help. Then, when the parent who has moved out calls, the child can hold the picture and talk or just listen. These phone conversations don't have to be lengthy. "I'm here. I'm your daddy. I love you," will suffice. Daily physical contact is better, however, and, if possible, it should last for thirty minutes to an hour.

If your child is old enough for overnight visitation, do send special security items back and forth—a favorite pillow, book, blanket, doll, or stuffed animal. These items represent constancy, something that is permanent and not lost. Try to keep nighttime and daycare routines the same to preserve as much continuity as possible for your toddler or youngster.

The level of animosity between parents is high at this stage of the divorce, but every effort should be made to be rational, mature, and focused on the child. For the sake of your child's sense of security, the relationship with the missing parent must be encouraged and not interfered with. If on the one hand you are telling him, "We both love you," yet, on the other hand you don't promote visitation with the parent who has moved out, you are indirectly making a contrary and confusing statement to your child.

"See You at Soccer, Dad"

Beginning at about age four, most children are involved in extracurricular activities, making it easier for parents who have moved out of the house to maintain supportive involvement. Also by this age, it's easier for children to be away from their mothers. So, depending upon the temperament of the child and the level of hostility in your divorce, you may have the ability to be flexible with visitation times. When you are making these decisions, think about what works best for your child—not what works best for you.

A week on–week off routine usually doesn't work for children unless the estranged spouses live very close to one another and have an amicable relationship. Kids with this type of visitation often complain about leaving behind friends when they go from one home to the next. Thursday through Monday visitation works well for some families. In this situation one parent has a child from the time school is out on Thursday through the weekend and takes the child to school on Monday. This keeps both parents involved with school. Still for other children, weekend-only visitation is best.

An initial separation time gives you a good opportunity to learn how to work together with your spouse. Consider your child's feelings, activities, and need for contact with both of you while making your decisions. If you can work through these issues now, permanent custody and visitation (see chapters 6 and 7) will be far simpler.

I encourage reading children's books about divorce to your children at bedtime or making up stories for younger children to help them get used to the idea of divorce and to begin working through issues. Make up a story about an animal whose parents get divorced, and let your child help tell the story by asking her what comes next or what the mommy or daddy says. Through stories and books you can talk about the issues that could be worrying your child— things like "Where am I going to sleep?" or "Will I have to share a room?"

Don't make a young child responsible for packing her bag to go visit nor give in to the temptation to "just let Dad buy everything" in order to hit him in the pocketbook. While forcing Dad to make these purchases may give Mom some satisfaction if she feels slighted economically, it also puts the child in the uncomfortable position of having to ask for basic things that should be provided. This will make your child feel uncomfortable, and often, she will choose to do without rather than ask. The best solution is to work together. Ask the other parent if he or she has the basics—toothbrush, pajamas, underwear, or if you need to send those each time.

"But I Have Plans..."

With teenagers, the important thing to remember is flexibility. Teenagers are going to be very involved with peer group activities and are not going to want to be bothered with visitation. Don't take it personally. Be more accommodating and less demanding of their time, and you'll be rewarded with their adjustment to this difficult situation. Dinner every Wednesday night and spending the night with one parent one weekend and one parent the next may not work with their busy social life. Respect that. Ask them what works for them. Try saying "yes" for a change. "Sure you can go to the party, but this is your weekend with me, so let's make some time for each other, too." You'll find that if you don't try to force the relationship, but instead leave options open, you'll master visitation even with a teenager.

Visitation doesn't work, however, when it is set up by the parents for the parents instead of for the kids. Parents do damage when they lose sight of what visitation is really all about—a new way of shared parenting. Too often parenting wasn't shared in the marriage, so when separation arrives, vengeful parents who felt overburdened in the marriage try to use visitation to show the other parent how hard their job has been. It's not uncommon for these vengeful types to set up doctor visits, dental visits, or other activities to keep the other parent running all over town during their visitation time. What the vengeful parent forgets is they are robbing their child of important time with the other parent.

Pushing off the responsibility for your child to "even the score with your ex" also creates insecurities in your child. When one parent has been the child's home base and source of stability, encouragement, support and nurturing, and then he is suddenly pushed on to a parent he has not been very connected with, it's difficult for him to handle. Shared parenting is a good thing, but if it is foreign to a child, ease him into it gradually.

"I Can't Do What *I* Want to Do Anymore"

"Gradual" is a good watchword when it comes to change and children. It's always best to introduce change gradually. But with divorce, gradual is sometimes impossible. Separation is sudden. Forced visitation is sudden. Realize how difficult this is on your children and help them cope. For kids, separation and visitation means a loss of control over their lives. Their schedules are now made—and often broken—at the whim of separated parents who have schedules that may conflict. They can no longer simply accept an invitation from a friend without going through a protracted process of finding out which parent they'll be with and then getting permission from the appropriate parent. They no longer have the freedom of spontaneity.

"I Love You Both"

Divorce for a child too often comes down to a division of loyalty and love between parents. If children are made to feel that they have to choose, it can tear them apart. When I ask a young child of divorce to draw a picture of her family, far too often she literally splits herself down the middle, being torn apart by the mother on one side and the father on the other. These graphic illustrations show how deeply they feel the pain.

Illustration 2: Boy, age 11, "I feel ripped in half."

Children's art is often much more expressive than words. The loyalty test is truly painful. This child is asking, "How can I love my dad when my mom hates my dad? How can I love my mom when my dad hates my mom?

Illustration 3: Girl, age 7, "I feel sawed down the middle."

The child is beginning to feel the tug of loyalty from her parents. She's getting ragged in the middle and calls her home life, "yucky."

Illustration 4: Boy, age 8, "They're pulling and my head's stuck in the middle."

This child feels no stability in his life. He doesn't even have a body. He is helpless. Life is this struggle for his head, and that's all.

Illustration 2

Illustration 3

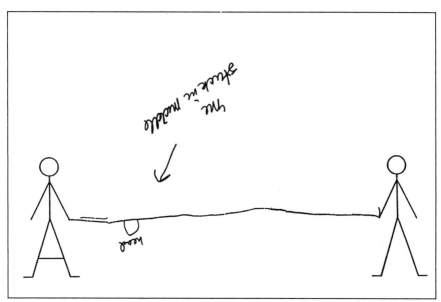

Illustration 4

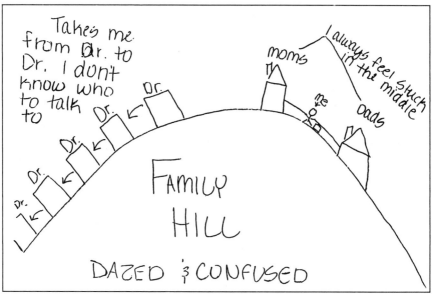

Illustration 5

Illustration 5: Girl, age 13, "I always feel stuck in the middle."

I asked this child to draw how it feels to be in a divorce situation. This young teenager lives with her father, but her mother is trying to regain custody by taking her from doctor to doctor to doctor looking for an opinion that will be favorable to her. The mother's pressure on the child has been extremely disturbing to the child and has resulted in at least one runaway episode to escape the constant discord.

Jimmy, nine, describes the pressure he feels from both parents for his loyalty as "ten times worse than the pressure of a major test in school." But unlike the stress of school exams, which comes and goes, the loyalty question from Jimmy's parents is a constant pressure.

To prevent your children from having to go through this painful experience, it's critical to make every attempt to get along in front of them now, from the beginning. At this time, soon after separation, your child's antennas are up. Children are looking for any reaction you might have to one another. And remember, as pointed out earlier, they see much more than you think they see.

It's easy for me to say "act happy" and hard for you to do it, because, indeed, this is far from a happy time. But this is the most important time for you to try to be decent to one another. Your child does not know yet how to love you both in this new separated family. Your child feels awkward expressing love for you both when you aren't loving, or even civil, toward one another. Your child doesn't want to take sides—so don't make him. Don't give in to the temptation to take your child aside and tell him your side of the story. That's the worst thing you could do now.

During this stage of divorce, it's easy for the two of you to forget that there was, in most cases, a point when everything was good between you. Usually it was during the good times when your child was conceived and born. Try to draw from those past experiences now to give you the power to be civil to one another.

You can't avoid the loyalty push and pull altogether, no matter what you do. Your job, however, is to try to minimize these feelings. Amy, now twenty-five, has been living between her divorced parents since high school. But even today, she says, she feels guilty leaving one behind when she visits the other. "If I go home at Mother's Day, I feel like I am leaving my father out and that he is going to get his feelings hurt because I'm not visiting him," she says.

The instinct of loyalty is deeply imprinted in us. We are not so far evolved from those clans that lived in caves. Since elementary school, we are taught that we are part of a group. If you are loyal to your clique of friends, you can't play with others outside the group; you have to alienate the outsiders. Kids are automatically programmed that way whether it seems right or not.

Put your own feelings aside and make the loyalty issue easier. Steve, ten, talks about how bad he felt when he got hurt at his soccer game and ran to his mother instead of his father for comfort. It was his dad's weekend, and his dad felt slighted and stormed off to the car. These episodes are tragic for children. When they do well at a game, they don't know who to run to first. Don't make them choose. If your child runs to the other parent, join him, and help celebrate. Don't get petty.

Kerry, seventeen, lost all of the joy she had felt at the end of her school play when her father and stepmother—sitting on the right side of the auditorium—presented her with flowers during a curtain call. Kerry felt responsible that her mom, sitting alone on the left side of the auditorium, was left out.

From the beginning remove the burden of guilt from your children. Before they assume that showing love for the other parent will hurt you, assure them it won't by promoting their relationship with the other parent. Before your child gets the chance to think, "I want to call my dad, but I don't want to hurt my mother's feelings," let him know it's okay with you any time he wants to call his dad.

Talk about the division of loyalty with your children. Get it out in the open. "It won't hurt my feelings if you have a good time with your dad." "I'm excited that you're looking forward to this special time with your mom." Give them permission to love both of their parents.

"Why Can't You Just Get Back Together?"

In this interim period before your divorce has really even begun, it's very natural for kids to hold out hope that you will get back together. Whether you had a stormy marriage or a good one that went bad, your child is going to have these feelings. You don't want to give your child false hope, but at the same time, if you are in counseling, don't shut the door on this possibility altogether. Just be honest and tell your child there are some adult issues between the two of you that you are working on, and you don't know what will happen.

But realize that if you sit together at the soccer game, laughing and joking, your child is going to hope for reconciliation. If that's not going to happen, be sure you communicate it clearly and strongly. Tell your child, "I know you want us to get back together again, but it's not going to happen." Or if your situation is hopeful, "I don't know what's going to happen. We are trying." Avoid the temptation to say things like, "I wanted to go to counseling but your mother/father wouldn't go." Don't set up situations that may give your children false hope or that put the blame for the relationship's failure on the other.

"This Is Just Weird"

Separation time is a pretty artificial time for kids. Neither parent is acting natural—toward one another or toward their children. Out of guilt, parents are usually more indulgent in an attempt to soothe their child's feelings. Instead, every effort should be made to keep life as normal as possible. Don't give in to the tendency to become a Walt Disney mom or dad.

Try to avoid the temptation to be nosy. Before your separation you didn't ask your child twenty questions when she walked in the door after an outing with the other parent. "Hi!" is an appropriate greeting for your child when she returns home from a weekend or outing with your spouse. "I missed you" makes your child feel guilty. When you go beyond a simple greeting, you're probably wanting to interrogate her to satisfy your own needs not hers. Why do you ask, "Did you have fun?" Are you really trying to get some dirt on your soon-to-be-ex?

Illustration 6: Boy, age 8, "When I come over he wants to know everything about my other house."

This child is being put under pressure by a parent who wants to know everything that's going on at the other parent's house. The result is this child has no privacy and strikes out against the too inquisitive parent. This child's father is literally trying to turn him into a spy to help gather damaging evidence against his own mother.

"Mom Asked Me to Ask You..."

During a divorce both parties start leading with their feelings and not with common sense. Parents overreact,

Illustration 6

misjudge, and forget what's best for their children. That's part of the reason why parents end up using their kids instead of raising their kids. During this initial period of separation, parents often use their children to communicate to their estranged spouse. This is unfairly hard on kids and puts them in a different role—an adult role that is not theirs.

Force yourself to have a conversation. Hand over a note. Leave a message on voice mail. But don't send your child as messenger—remember what happens to the bearers of bad news. Your children are fragile little characters who didn't make this divorce happen. Keep them out of the fray from the start.

5

The Process of Divorce—"My Mommy and Daddy Are Getting a Divorce"

THE LEGAL SYSTEM is far from child-friendly. As you begin the legal journey through the family court system, your child will learn a whole new vocabulary filled with imposing adult words like divorce, attorney, guardian *ad litem*, social worker, and judge's chambers. Depending upon the volatility of your divorce and the laws and guidelines in your community, your family may have to go through a lengthy process of evaluation by social workers and psychologists—yet another foreign and artificial world to your child.

This is a time filled with risk when parents can easily lose control of their children's destiny by relying on attorneys and judges to make decisions that parents should be making. The family court system is adversarial, and many attorneys thrive on this battleground. Some attorneys don't hesitate to bring up custody as a tool to enhance their client's position in the economic arena of the divorce.

"Mommy, Whose Fault Is It?"

The divorce process is difficult for parents. It's now open season on the life two parents have shared, which is filled with memories, both good and bad. Mistakes made on both sides are turned into threats and weapons to obtain desired conditions through the divorce. Though Oklahoma became the first state to adopt no-fault divorce in the 1950s, and, since that time, every state has followed suit, many attorneys still manage to place blame on their client's spouse in an effort to win the advantage in court.

No-fault divorce eliminated the need to prove that one party was responsible for the failure of the marriage, but it did nothing to soften the adversarial system where child custody is concerned. While you and your attorneys search for dirt to try to sway a court's custody decision, remember, your child will be doing the same. More often than not, your child will place blame on himself. This is a time to be especially careful with your words and your anger and where you shed your tears. Little eyes and ears are watching and listening closely. Reaffirm the message for your children that they in no way caused this divorce or your ongoing anger or sadness over it. Let your children know that you are sad about the divorce, but avoid placing blame on your spouse or his or her lawyer.

Your child will be angry about the divorce, too. When you heap anger and abuse on your spouse, you give your child permission to do the same. If you are thrilled when your child gets angry with your ex, remember what your reaction teaches them. Aren't you indirectly teaching your child to disrespect authority? Proceed with caution here: If you sow the seeds of disrespect for one parent now, you run the risk of reaping the harvest in your own home one day. Although it is natural for you and your child to look for someone to blame for your anger, you'll be better served if you try to steer your child's anger toward the situation and away from the players. While your arguments during marriage may have been about everything from shared household duties to adultery, your arguments during and after divorce will most likely be about money and the children—the two issues you still have in common. Even discussions about money will likely be related to your children—for instance, school tuition, or the cost of extracurricular activities. These things may not have been stipulated in a temporary support agreement. So, it's no wonder kids blame themselves for divorce when they overhear angry words that relate directly to them.

Before you bring up these subjects in front of your child, stop and think about how your conversations will make him feel. It should be your goal to foster a good relationship between your child and the other parent. This is the best thing for him in the long run—to be loved by, and to love, two parents.

Your child will be asking you tough questions during this stage of your divorce. But you should be asking some tough ones of yourself. Remember, with most attorneys, this split is all about money and how much you and they will get. When it's all over, and the equivalent of your child's college education is now in your attorney's bank account, will it be worth it? Are you risking your child's future by trying to punish your ex-partner? Are you fanning the flames of your divorce in order to get in one last hurtful dig?

"Are We Divorced Yet?"

Though no-fault divorce cuts down on the time it takes to get a divorce, some states still have lengthy waiting periods that can exacerbate this painful time for your child. In

California, parents have to wait six months for a divorce; in New York, a year. But in the most hostile divorces, attorneys will institute their own delays, dragging out the process to exhaust their opponents.

As a tool, delay can wear down even the most energetic opposition. But if you allow the battle to be prolonged, realize you are also upping the ultimate price of your divorce—in terms of both dollars and the emotional health of your children. Delay is damaging because usually the relationship between parents degenerates during this time since nothing has been resolved. It is normal for parents to become depressed while they're in limbo, and this negativity makes for a horrible environment for kids. Children—and parents—can't begin to heal as long as the situation is without a satisfactory resolution.

Custody arrangements have the potential to be in place within three months. However, I've seen them drag on for more than a year before both parties could come to an agreement. Remember how long time stretched from summer vacation until Christmas when you were a child? Your concept of time is very different now, isn't it? Doesn't Christmas seem to sneak up on you these days? Don't the years fly by? But a year is still forever to a child.

Unresolved conflicts aren't always about money. I've seen parents drag out custody battles over what church their children are going to attend, what school they will attend, how they will spend their time off from school, and, of course, visitation schedules. But increasingly, I've found the fights are parent driven not attorney driven. The hostility and selfishness are overwhelming. As parents you spend the first four years of your child's life teaching him to share. But as so often happens when parents become embattled, they don't know how to share something so important as a human life.

"Do You and Daddy Have the Same Lawyer?"

Choosing the right attorney is the best thing you can do to protect your child. Start by interviewing an attorney whose major focus is family practice. Ask how long it typically takes the attorney to settle a divorce case like yours and if the attorney is in favor of mediation (more about mediation later). Be wary of attorneys who want to go for the kill. Depending upon the circumstances of your separation, this could be very tempting. You must realize, however, that a prolonged, all-out war between you and your spouse *will* damage the relationship your child has with you and his other parent and can do long-term harm to him. Never forget that your child loves both you and your spouse. It hurts him to watch you be hateful to one another.

Be sure to interview several different attorneys who specialize in family law. Ask for an attorney who has had experience as a guardian *ad litem* for children. These attorneys will have at least worked from a child's perspective in the past, so they should know how to put children first in a divorce.

If your lawyer is hostile and you are hostile, it will be next to impossible to keep your child from being negatively affected. Some attorneys in difficult divorce situations automatically recommend restricting access to the other parent until temporary visitation orders are in place. In cases where you suspect the other parent might try to leave the state or country with the child, this may be good advice. But in most cases, it only starts the process of using the child to threaten or punish the other parent, setting the stage for parental alienation—which can be far more damaging to your child than to your ex.

Again, three months is a reasonable guideline for resolving

custody and support issues. Property issues may take longer to resolve, but if you get the custody and support issues out of the way, the property issues will be greatly simplified. Attorneys will no longer have custody or support to use as leverage. In other words, you have focused exclusively on your child and then taken him out of the picture so that he can't be used one way or the other. How civilized! And how healthy for all involved. After all, isn't your child the most valuable asset you and your spouse have? Shouldn't she get special attention first and foremost? Together you did want to have a child, didn't you?

If you do find that you are in a war and can't change the tone of the divorce, then immediately approach your lawyer to get a guardian *ad litem* attorney for your child. This will cost both you and your spouse more money and, as a result, may act as a motivation to settle the custody dispute more quickly. If the battle drags on, however, while you and your spouse and your respective attorneys lose perspective, the *ad litem* attorney will protect your child.

Parents at this stage of divorce often have a great need to punish one another. They get tunnel vision and forget that what they are doing has a great effect on their children. This is a time when parents will break down and grill their children for information, looking for ammunition to use against their spouses in the battle. Children are smart—they know when their parents are being sincerely concerned and when they're being nosy. This is the type of parental behavior that puts children in an impossible position in dealing with their parents. If you're playing these destructive games, you can bet your spouse is too. So stop. Think about your child. Remember, it is your job to preserve her relationship with both parents throughout this process and in the future. Study after study has shown that this is what is healthiest for her.

I've had kids tell me their parents have asked what kind of movie their mother or father took them to, what they ate over the weekend, were they left with a baby-sitter, and did their mother or father have a "friend" come along? All of these questions have ulterior motives. Would you have asked your child these questions with such interest if you had just returned from a business trip?

Joann, twelve, says that even when she wants to talk about one parent with her other parent, she feels conflicted. Is she going to hurt her daddy if she tells her mom they just hung out and watched videos all weekend? Is she going to hurt her mommy if she tells daddy they went shopping since they are always arguing about money?

"What's Mediation?"

I recommend trying mediation early on in the divorce process for a number of reasons. When you try mediation sooner rather than later, you have a much greater chance for compromise before each of you determines a position and stubbornly sticks to it. If mediation works, it will shorten the divorce process by many months since you will be working toward a settlement rather than a potential trial to dispose of your case.

Mediation limits the time involvement of lawyers, which means it's cheaper than a prolonged divorce battle. In this controlled environment, where your interests are still protected by your attorney, you can explore the possibilities of your post-divorce family without too much risk. In mediation, parents still have control over their children's and their own destinies. Who should better know what's best for your child than you and his other parent? Do the attorneys, judge or, heaven forbid, jury love your child and know him as the two of you do?

Perhaps the biggest plus of mediation is that it can help divorcing parents learn how to work together to determine what's best for their children. This is good practice for the rest of your lives as a split family. If you can learn to find common ground in parenting your child while you divorce, you will be far ahead of where you would be coming out of a hostile custody battle. If you learn how to resolve issues about your child together now, you will probably be able to avoid returning to the court to decide upon issues that come up in the future after your divorce is final, thus saving thousands of dollars.

If you still need extra incentive to try mediation, visualize what your attorney's hourly fees could buy your child. That new soccer uniform and team dues. Braces. Therapy for the whole family. That first car. Family vacations. A college education.

Remember, your relationship with your spouse will be ongoing anyway. The definition of divorce only means that you are no longer married to one another. With a child involved, you will never be "free" from contact with this person. And, most importantly, your child is not divorcing either you or your spouse.

"Do I Get to Talk to the Judge?"

I strongly discourage bringing your child directly into the divorce process by either putting her on the stand or allowing her to be questioned by the judge in chambers. It can be extremely damaging to your child to put her in a position where she feels she has to choose between parents. Inevitably, a small child brought into this situation will think she is "on trial" or in trouble and has done something wrong.

The system can, however, gather information from your

child in less harmful ways. Judges can order psychological evaluations, studies of home environments, or appoint guardian *ad litem* attorneys to represent children's interests and, in essence, speak for the children in the court room. Remember, this is an adversarial system and you don't want to subject your child to a process where she could feel attacked by improper questioning. This is a very artificial situation for a child and one where it is difficult for her to have to be honest and open. Here is this person who to a child is ten feet tall, cloaked in black, bending over in her face and asking questions. This is not to say that a lot of judges aren't kind and sympathetic to children, but children perceive the situation as scary. They feel at risk of alienating the two people they love the most—their mother and father. It's a deeply agonizing position for a child to be in.

Beginning at about age twelve, children are asked by some family court judges for their input about visitation and custody arrangements. Even at this age, when a child may be somewhat familiar with the workings of a courtroom through television and movies, you should encourage that questioning by the judge be in private and in the judge's chambers. Approach this with caution, however, because if one parent is unhappy with the judge's decision, the child is going to feel guilty and responsible for the pain caused.

"Why Are We Getting a Divorce?"

How much should you tell your children about the reasons behind and the progress of your divorce? As little as possible. Very young children, five years old and younger, aren't developmentally capable of understanding the concepts of divorce. Follow the guidelines in chapter 4, "Separation." Both of you explain to your child that Mommy and Daddy think it's best to not be married anymore. Then reassure him that no one is leaving him, that he will always have a mommy and daddy who love him even though Mommy and Daddy will live in two houses now.

By the time he reaches school age, both of you sit down with your child and tell him that the two of you have adult problems you can't solve, and some other people, called attorneys and a judge, are going to help you get a divorce and solve those problems. Clarify again and again—every time you get the chance—that the problems have nothing to do with him.

With adolescents and teenagers, after you've told them you are getting a divorce, let the news sink in and then respond to their questions only with limited information. Both of you want to continue in your positions as parent, and the more you tell your child about what is going on with your divorce, the more you move the child up into the position of being a cohort or ally. Older children need to live on neutral ground during and after divorce. Don't make them feel like they are being loyal to one parent and disloyal to the other by telling them about your attorney's latest dirty trick.

Don't tell your child that Daddy/Mommy is trying to take him away from you—even if this is true. You'll only be setting your child up for a life of pain, guilt, and regret.

It's important to listen to your child during the process of your divorce, because there is a tendency for many parents to become wrapped up in self-pity to the exclusion of all else. But it is also important to listen to yourself. How do you sound from the perspective of your child? Do you give him mixed messages? "I want you to love your daddy, but I don't love him any more." Do you tell your child you want him to respect your spouse, then in the next breath complain that you can't afford anything because your spouse won't give you any money? Do you follow your attorney's lead, mistrust your spouse, and then confuse your child with that message. "I want you to see your mom, but you have to have a baby-sitter with you." "I want you to see your dad, but we have to have permission from the judge." "Honey, I would be at home with you tonight but your mother wanted me to go." "I would love to be at your game, but your dad doesn't want me to come." "I wish I could call you every night, but you'll have to ask your mom if that's okay."

Use common sense. If you let yourself make comments like these, and attempt to alienate the other parent, it will only backfire on you later. Your child will blame you and will resent you for denying him this important primary relationship. If you can avoid peppering your information about your child's other parent with innuendoes and sarcasm right now, that would be the healthiest way to get the child through your divorce. When in doubt *we* is always a good word to use to answer your child's tough questions about divorce. When you begin the sentence with we, it's hard to trash your spouse or place blame.

If there are serious issues of abuse or neglect, act immediately to protect your child. That's the first priority. However, you can still accomplish this without being negative about the other parent to your child. At the Family Connection, counselors teach parents positive ways to interact with their children through education, guidance, and supervision. We see some of the most extreme cases of neglect, abuse, and problematic divorce. Here children can have access to parents who have been alienated for a variety of reasons or who can't be trusted alone with their children. Parents who can't get along well enough to have a civil exchange of their children can drop kids off here for pickup by the other parent. At the Family Connection, we teach both parents the importance of a child's right to two parents. Here angry parents learn how to talk to their children in a healthier way. "Your dad/mom needs some help right now to learn how to be a good parent." "Your mom/dad has made some mistakes, but he/she is taking some lessons, and we think it will be okay again someday for you to visit him/her."

Allegations of sexual abuse have been widely used in recent years against both fathers and mothers in custody battles. What some attorneys call the "neutron bomb of custody fights" is now dropped with amazing frequency. Dr. Kathleen Faller, a University of Michigan sociologist, believes, based on her studies of the subject, that one in three allegations of sexual abuse during divorce are impossible to prove or are false. Other experts say as many as 80 percent of these claims have no basis in fact.[2]

Fathers of very young children are in a tough position. When a toddler gets diaper rash and goes home and tells mom, "Daddy touched my bottom and it hurt," a mother filled with hatred will think the worst. I had one child whose father was accused of inappropriate touching of his daughter when she was four years old. Five years later, the father has been through counseling, and the court thinks it is a good time for the father and daughter to begin to see one another again. There have been day visits, but no overnights. When I asked the child what would make her feel safe and comfortable, she says she just wants her father to apologize and then never bring it up again. She can't remember any abuse, and the father has always denied it. Meanwhile, this relationship was completely interrupted for several years. The child, who is now perhaps too well versed about abuse, is not afraid, and only wants to have a more normal relationship with her father.

Another prime time for false allegations of abuse is when unhappy adolescents are searching for a way out of a tight spot. Stephanie, a seventh grader, had lived with her father for two years. When she was caught stealing at a convenience store, her father lost it and slapped her. In a minute she was on the phone to her maternal grandmother who called Child Protective Services (CPS), which in turn removed Stephanie from her home. For the next four months while CPS investigated the case, Stephanie was moved from relative to relative, all the while wishing to go home to her father, who was in a vulnerable position as an opposite-sex single parent.

Sexual maturation can be negatively affected by divorce. As you grow up, you develop your sexual identity by watching your parents interact. You learn about relationships, healthy and unhealthy, from them. In some respect this explains the passing of violence and various forms of abuse from generation to generation. Girls begin to think that as an adult they need to be submissive and take criticism and verbal abuse. Boys, watching their mother's get attacked, lose respect for them and project this view onto other females.

Divorce brings the primary relationship model in a child's life to an end and introduces the possibility of other adults as sexual partners for parents. This is a tough area for kids and parents alike. The issue of parents remarrying is dealt with in greater detail in chapter 9.

"Did Daddy/Mommy Divorce Us?"

To children, divorce is rejection—rejection of them. Since children see themselves as the center of the world, they naturally think they are the object of the divorce. What adults do not understand is that, for children, divorce is unending. Parents may be able to divorce one another, emotionally recover, and "start a new life." But children will live with the divorce for the rest of their lives and will continue to look for love and support from both parents whether the parents are there for them or not.

When your divorce becomes final, you will probably experience a general letdown that is an uneasy blend of loss and relief. Don't be tempted to turn to your children for comfort. Anthony, twelve, a mature child, was really curious about the divorce procedure and asked to go along with his mother to court when the final papers were signed. There was no ulterior motive in letting him go. But with most children, there's no need to commemorate the divorce in some way or even to communicate to them that it's final unless that finality is going to bring about some immediate change in living arrangements. For your kids, you were divorced the day one parent moved out of the house.

That doesn't mean your child has "accepted" your divorce. Emotionally your child is going to go through a lot of transitions—from grief, loss, depression, and numbness to the refusal to accept that this is permanent. I have heard kids whose parents have been divorced for many years say they want their parents back together again. They'll hold onto this hope for as long as they can because children want a whole home, not a broken home.

6

Custody—"Where Will I Live?"

TO CHILDREN, the notion of "custody" is not only artificial, it's just plain weird. They love both of their parents, and the concept of "belonging" to one versus the other doesn't make any sense. The word custody itself implies ownership, so it's no wonder that many parents take an attitude that the child needs to be the possession of one or the other parent now that the marriage is dissolving. The terminology used to describe what happens to families after a divorce is part of the problem. Some states have begun to change their use of adversarial terms like "custody order" to the more cooperative sounding "parenting plan." "Noncustodial" parents can be called "nonresidential," for instance.

The U.S. Commission on Child and Family Welfare, in making recommendations to the courts for dealing with divorce, writes that terms like custody and visitation should be replaced with terms that are "less likely to foster conflict such as 'parental decision-making,' 'parenting time,' and 'residential arrangements' for children."[3]

Commission member Bill Harrington, in his minority

report to the commission, passionately elaborates on this point, "'Visitation' is a tragic word which undermines the very fragile parental relationship, trust, bonding and authority that a noncustodial parent/child already has. Allowing the use of this term to apply to children engaged in parenting time with their 'noncustodial' parent is harmful. The child lives ALSO at the other home, and is not *just* a visitor."[4]

More positive language may be a step in the right direction to help parents avoid behaviors that can hurt their children. But parents must learn to hold their hostile behavior in check and recognize that raising a child together is a lifetime commitment that will not end when divorce papers are signed. You're in it together. Make it a smooth ride for your children. After all, arguing about the language used to describe divorce is an adult issue. Children don't call it "custody" or "visitation" anyway. They are likely to ask you simply, "When can I see my mom/dad?" The correct answer should be, "Whenever you want to."

Unlike dividing property, splitting up a child is simply impossible. You can't divide a child the way you divide wedding gifts or furniture. However, parents who now hate one another will try, and, as a result, make a child feel split right down the middle. It sounds painful, and it is.

There are many types of custody arrangements. A court can award sole custody to one parent, joint custody to both parents, or divided (sometimes called split) custody, where each parent has custody of one or more children. It's important to understand that legal custody (decision-making power) and physical custody (where the children live) are two distinct issues. Visitation is also a separate issue, discussed in the next chapter.

Sole or exclusive custody gives one parent the power to make decisions about how the child or children will be brought up—including issues such as education, health care, and or religion. Joint or shared custody gives that decision-making power to both parents. Divided or split custody can give each parent that power with regard to the child in his or her physical custody or can give both parents joint legal custody while dividing physical custody. Where the children live or how and when they see the other parent can vary greatly from family to family.[5]

Infants and toddlers don't need to be told anything about the legal ramifications of custody. Toddlers only need to know that they are going to be with daddy and mommy on a regular basis—but not together. Children and preadolescents also need only know that Mommy and Daddy will still be making decisions together even though they are divorced. If one parent or the other is given custody of a teenager, the teenager does need to know who has legal responsibility and who will be making decisions about his or her welfare. This may help prevent the teenager from trying to manipulate parents by playing one off against the other. However, handling a teenager is hard enough even if divorce is not complicating the situation. If you can, present a united front to keep your teen in bounds.

Support—a very important issue for both the custodial, or residential, parent and noncustodial, or nonresidential parent—is determined in a number of ways and varies according to jurisdictions. In the 1988 Family Support Act, child support guidelines were mandated for all states. Determining factors include the number of children, the income earned by each spouse, and the amount of time the children spend with each parent.[6]

There'll be more discussion of this subject in both the next chapter on visitation and in chapter 8, "The New Standard of Living," but the important thing for parents to remember is that child support is not something children need to hear about. It's an adult issue. They don't need to know how much it is, that it's late, that it's behind. They don't need to know that Daddy's money bought the Christmas presents or paid the school tuition or the house payment, or that Mommy's money bought the groceries or the school clothes or the toys. All they need to know is that Mommy and Daddy are always going to take care of them, even though they aren't married any more. Period.

The 50-50 Share

Judges today often find the easiest "division" of the children is fifty-fifty joint custody. But in many cases, I strongly caution against this solution. Joint custody, with true fifty-fifty share parenting, is successful only if the parents have a good relationship and live close enough to one another for the school and neighborhood to be the same. Only then can they actually work together for the best interest of the children.

Think about how many divorced couples you know who have a good relationship. I'll bet you can count them on one hand. In my twenty years of professional experience, I have known of only two satisfactory joint parenting relationships. One is a colleague and spouse who have been successful at putting aside their feelings about each other to bring up three healthy children—two now in college and one finishing up high school. For the ten years since they divorced, they have been able to attend school conferences together and make important decisions about the needs of their children by discussing them and coming to a joint decision.

Their visitation arrangement was rotated—one week with one parent, the next week with the other parent. This schedule worked because the parents lived fairly close to one another.

Why does joint custody so often fail? The answer is obvious: for the same reasons the marriage failed. Parents often divorce because they can't get along and because they disagree on major issues affecting their children. Even if they could make decisions together while they were married, after a prolonged custody battle, working together can be asking the impossible. If parents couldn't make decisions together or get along before they were divorced, how are they miraculously supposed to work together amicably afterward? What often ensues is a relationship where parents have to run back to the court for decisions they haven't been able to make together, often spending more money on legal fees year after year to the detriment of the children's financial position.

In addition, many parents assume if they get joint custody there will be no child support payments. This is true only if the parents' incomes are the same and the children spend equal time with both parents.

"Who Do I Ask for Permission?"

From the perspective of the child, joint custody is far from a panacea. A child who goes back and forth between parents and whose parents are supposed to share decision making is often in a tough position when asking permission for special activities or even when making simple requests for clothing items. Since the parents are supposed to be working together, major purchases or special events need to be discussed. But since the parents no longer share a household, the logistics are more complicated, often resulting in a long waiting period for an answer. This is frustrating to kids and can prompt them to keep such questions to themselves, either opting out of activities altogether or waiting until the last minute to pop the question, thus forcing the issue.

If parents do get along—or can learn to get along when it comes to their child—then joint custody is absolutely the best situation. Joint custody gives a child permission to be truly attached to both parents without hurting either's feelings. This should be the goal of every custody situation and clearly is what's best for the child.

"Who Will Buy?"

Divorce sets up the opportunity for kids to manipulate parents, and parents, trying to get the loyalty edge, may try to "buy love." The best solution here for the parent who is not willing to resort to checkbook warfare is to be constant and consistent with your own rules and rewards at your household. Try to instill the concept of waiting and saving for rewards from your end. Remember, you can't control what happens at your ex's house, only at your own. Indeed this is a very threatening type of warfare, especially with younger children who are very materialistic. But if your conviction is to teach values, your child will eventually realize when gifts are a bribe and when they are truly gifts.

"Are We Getting Back Together?"

A brief word of caution for parents who do get along well. Don't go overboard and encourage your child's secret wish that you will reunite. Yes, be civil, considerate, even caring. But don't go out and have dinner together or socialize in a way that could be perceived by your child as dating. Although your child may always wish that you will get back together again, you don't want to give her false hope by being overly inclusive of your ex.

Not Too Close

Some children have a need to keep the people and things

in their two houses separate. If a child closes the door in his mother's face when she comes to pick him up at his father's house, he's not being rude. He doesn't want to comingle these two parts of his life. Kids know their parents will make snide remarks, so letting each side know very little about the other is one technique the kids use to avoid hearing the negatives.

Remember, there's no right or wrong way for your child to deal with this new and strange parental relationship. You are all searching for what's comfortable for your child given his or her unique temperament.

Sole or Divided Custody

If you and your spouse can't reasonably make decisions together, it's probably best for the judge to assign responsibility. Again, the variations are endless. I've seen judge's give decision-making powers regarding education to one parent and health care to another. When it comes to deciding where the child's primary residence will be, the judge will try to determine which parent provides the most stable situation, psychologically and emotionally, for the child.

It doesn't matter who makes the most money, but rather who the child is most attached to on a consistent basis. One tool I use when evaluating psychological attachment for custody cases is to ask a child to draw himself with each parent, separately and together. The following illustrations show how attachment to a parent can vary from strong to a more vague association.

Illustration 7: Girl, age 7
The parents of this child argued quite a bit in front of her before the divorce began. These arguments usually resulted in the mother crying. In this drawing, it's apparent that this little

Illustration 7

Illustration 8

girl is trying to protect her mom. The father's display of temper has served to make her more dependent on her mom and pushed her into a caretaking role. The lesson here is that parents must not belittle each other in front of their children. This illustration shows in a visual way what happens when they do. If you demean your ex, it will not make your child more loyal to you, but will instead make your child feel like he or she needs to take care of the object of your criticism.

Illustration 8: Boy, age 8

This child has drawn himself with his arms wrapped around his father's waist. The illustration shows what happens when a mother tries to keep a child away from a father that he is strongly attached to. This child was becoming pretty depressed while he lived with his mother. He was showing moodiness in school and crying a lot. He only had weekend visitation with his father and for him, this wasn't enough. In this child's case, the court and the mother didn't recognize the depth of the bond the child had with his father. When there is a very strong bond with one parent, that must be considered in the custody evaluation and by the parents as they assess their own behavior. I recommended a change of residence for this child. Now he is happy living with his father and is very successful in school. He sees his mother once during the week and every other weekend, and for now, that is enough for him.

Illustration 9: Boy, age 11

In this child's family, prior to the divorce, the father had become the primary caretaker of the children. This boy's mother was a professional who had a very demanding job. She left early each morning and came home late each night. She was also having an affair and, though the kids never knew about that, they felt her emotional absence from the home.

Illustration 9

Illustration 10

The father's business, however, allowed him to work out of the home. On a daily basis, he was more available for the kids. As the parents drifted apart and their marriage came to an end, without an undue amount of anger in the home, I was called in to help decide upon custody. It became immediately apparent that the caretaking of the dad had made an impact on the little boy. He was much more attached to his father. The first time he drew himself with his parents, he put himself in the middle. Then he thought about it, erased, and drew himself closer to his dad.

Illustration 10: Boy, age 9

Although the mother in this divorce situation did not work outside the home, she was grieving so deeply over the failure of her marriage that she was completely unavailable to her children. When the son drew his family, he drew himself and his siblings with the father and Mom out by herself, away and detached. When I considered the best interests of the children, they were much better off with their father while their mother suffered from depression. When Mom gets better, and is emotionally available for her children again, residential and visitation arrangements may change.

Illustration 11: Boy, age 11

I told this little boy that the stick figure on the paper was his father and asked him to draw himself anywhere on this piece of paper. He drew himself as far away from his dad as he could and still be on the paper.

When this child was five years old, his father had a nervous breakdown. During that process, his mother filed for divorce. Due to his own suffering mental health, the father was absent from his child's life for about three years. During that time the bond with his mother grew incredibly strong.

Illustration 11

Illustration 12

The boy became the "man of the house," and essentially replaced his father.

Illustration 12: Boy, age 11
This is the same child as in Illustration 11. I told him, "Here's your mom and your dad. Put yourself on this same piece of paper." As you can see, he's drawn himself in an equal role with his mother and father, but he's with the mother—in the position you would expect a child to draw a husband and wife.

Divorce can set up this type of surrogate husband role for a child if parents aren't very careful to prevent a child from becoming a caretaker. Out of loneliness and fear of getting back into social situations, mothers and fathers will often substitute their children. "You'll be my date to the barbecue." In this case, the mother had essentially "dated" her son for the three years his father was absent. Their bond was so strong that there was no room for the father in the child's life at this point.

When the father sought a relationship, the child flatly refused. On judge's orders, we tried three encounters with the father and each was disastrous. We decided not to force the situation at this point to prevent further damage to the father-son relationship.

Illustration 13: Boy, age 11
This is what the same child drew when I told him, "Here's your mom. Put yourself somewhere."

Illustration 14: Boy, age 11
Here's how the same child drew his family—Mom and me. Moms have to be really careful, especially early on in separation, because children will often see them as vulnerable.

Illustration 13

Illustration 14

Parents should make a child feel he is important, but during a divorce, this message can get confused. Attachments can become too strong. I have to wonder how this extreme bond with a mother is going to affect this child's social and sexual development in the future. At only eleven years old, he sees himself on equal ground with his mom—there is no adult caretaker in his life.

Illustration 15: Boy, age 8

In this family prior to divorce, the father physically abused the mother. The child has drawn himself hiding behind his mom, afraid of his dad because while they were married the child saw so much physical aggression. Even though the violence was directed toward the mother, this boy was afraid he would get the same kind of treatment. So that he could continue a safe relationship with his father, supervised visits were recommended. Supervision was eventually relaxed; however, the father later abused the child, so all visitation was stopped.

Illustration 16: Girl, age 9

This drawing was made by the sister of the boy above. Her fears were very similar to her brother's. She drew herself as far away as she could from her father. Notice that her hands and feet are drawn in detail—ready for action to defend herself in case her father tries to hurt her.

Illustration 17: Boy, age 8

In this divorced family, the kids spent a week with their mom and the alternate week with their dad. As time went on, the children were happier with their father. This little boy has drawn himself waving good-bye to his mother. Further investigation revealed that the mother was constantly making

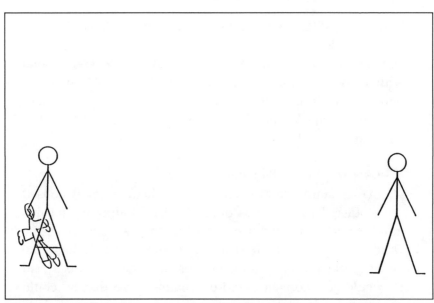

Illustration 15

Illustration 16

Illustration 17

Illustration 18

passive-aggressive, derogatory comments about the father—some more subtle than others, but none missed by the children. "I would love to buy you that, but your dad has not paid his child support." "I would like to be able to take you on vacation, too, but your dad makes more money than I do." "I would love to buy a bigger house, but your dad took all of our money."

Illustration 18: Boy, age 8

Propaganda against your ex is rarely, if ever, successful. This is the same child who is now sticking his tongue out at his mom and walking to his dad. You can't solicit your child's support in this battle of wills between parents. It will backfire on you every time. When you're angry, it's easy for bitterness to leak out in negative comments about your ex. But this will only hurt your relationship with your child.

When I try to help the courts decide custody, one of the things I consider is which parent is trying to support an attachment with the other parent. The kids with the most problems are the ones where neither parent promotes a relationship with the other. the kids who do best have at least one parent who is supportive of their seeing their other parent.

Illustration 19: Boy, age 8

Because his mother was so unsupportive of his relationship with his father, this child's response was, "No matter what you say, I want to be with my dad."

Illustration 20: Girl, age 9

This comic strip, if you will, was the way this little girl showed me what happened in her family's divorce. The divorce is final and she is leaving her mom's house, getting in

Illustration 19

Illustration 20

the car, and her custody is changing over to her dad. The child is very unemotional about the move. It is very matter-of-fact. In this family, the mother, newly separated, decided it was time to play. She tried to rationalize her behavior to her children, but all they could understand was that she was gone, and she was leaving them with various people in her absence. Her behavior bordered on neglect, so the dad got custody. Since the mother was already emotionally absent, the move did not produce feelings of being torn between the households.

When determining psychological attachment, sexual stereotypes must be put aside. Lisa, for example, a mother of two, was the family's primary breadwinner while her husband, Jim, was the parent involved in the children's day-to-day activities. He was the parent who left work when his kids were sick, took them to doctor's appointments, and tucked them in at night. Lisa's job was her priority, and her attitude toward parenting was much like a stereotypical father of the 1950s—she loved her kids but she fit in parenting only after her work was done. She was a breadwinner not a bread maker. Jim was the primary nurturer. The children were clearly his first priority. Both parents loved their children, but when determining where the kids should live, my recommendation to the judge was that Jim was truly their psychological parent.

This is not to say that children can go without their mothers. Infants, especially, need to keep in close contact with their moms in order to progress. A best-case scenario when parents with very young children divorce would allow mothers with the desire to be the residential parent to do so. They can develop their relationship with a child until at least age three and a half or four, when the child begins to show independence. Until this age it is much more difficult to explain to a child that Mommy is leaving the house than it is to explain that Daddy is leaving. There are studies supporting both sides of this issue, but I like to point to nature. In the early rearing of young animals, there is very little involvement of the male of the species. The males often take part in rearing only if the mother has been killed. This point, however, should not be used to rule out frequent contact by a father. The father, in order to ensure healthy attachment, should be with his infant daily, if possible, for at least an hour. Intense hostility makes this opportunity not only uncomfortable, but stressful for adults. It's worth the effort, however, if you hope to raise your child to be happy, healthy, and well adjusted.

After age four I believe both fathers and mothers can do equally well in the role of residential parent. I have four girl patients who are being raised by their dads who are doing very well. During adolescence, these girls may need a same-sex role model. If their dads can't get their daughters that influence from their exes, I will encourage them to make an effort to find another feminine influence for them.

A dad might start taking his daughter to the beauty shop, for instance, or find a dress store with a helpful saleswoman who will work with his daughter and help her select clothes. There are also classes given by department stores that teach makeup techniques, hair styling, and how to work with clothes styles. Children at this age are naturally anxious about their appearance and need a role model to help them know how to dress and how to act.

A mother might look to her brother or a male friend of the family to do "guy stuff" with her teenage son if Dad's not around. Or look into a Big Brother program, or something similar, at a church, synagogue, or community center.

"No One Has Time for Me Anymore"

Sometimes the custody arrangement you battled over in court ends up having a negative effect on everyone. In Dorothy's case, she fought hard for the majority of residential time with her children. Their father saw the kids only on alternating weekends and for dinner on Wednesday nights. Suddenly Dorothy found herself resentful and angry. She had all of the responsibility and no relief.

What does this mean for the kids? They're left with two angry parents: a dad who wouldn't help when he was asked because he felt unfairly treated by the courts, and a mother who had no patience with her children on a daily basis because she was tired and angry. Then Dad started dating and Mom got even more angry. When did she have the time for a social life? Now when those alternating weekends roll around, she's ready to play, and her kids feel they're being run out the door while she slips on her high heels. No wonder children feel dehumanized by divorce—more like objects tossed between houses. It's a horrible scenario for all, so when you're scheming with your lawyer to "get custody," think ahead.

"Why Can't You Just Be Nice to Each Other?"

No matter how hard you try, the odds are against your managing an amicable divorce. In my experience, even if divorces start out that way, the process of divorce itself is cruel and unusual punishment that will beat the civility out of even the most well-meaning couple. Marriages are filled with feelings and memories. Divorce court tries to put them on paper and then tear them in half. It doesn't work.

As the conflict between parents grows, the child becomes an object that is traded back and forth, and possession of that object becomes each parent's quest. I've seen parents who go back to court to decide who gets to pick a child up from summer camp. In some of the worst divorces, parents bring the custody battle down to counting the number of hours a child spends with each parent. Think about the language you use with one another. You talk about "trading weekends," "swapping holidays." Your child has become a commodity and don't think she doesn't feel it.

Try reversing that idea of ownership. Think about your situation as if your child is the owner and you and your ex belong to your child. Changing your thinking is a first step toward changing your behavior. If you can't change your behavior, get help soon or your kids will need it later.

7

Visitation—"When Do I Go to My Other House?"

LOOKING HARD FOR SOMETHING POSITIVE to say about divorce, thirteen-year-old Stephanie, whose parents have been apart since she was four, says that children of divorce get to spend more one-on-one time with their parents. "You get to know both your mom and your dad better than kids whose parents are married," she says.

This is a very insightful observation and one of the few positives about growing up in a split family. Stephanie's point underscores the importance of maintaining relationships with both parents—which is what "visitation" is all about. Visitation is not about giving the primary residential parent a break. It's not what a nonresidential parent "pays for" with child support. It's not about finding the most convenient arrangement for the parents. It's about children maintaining two healthy parental relationships. The best way to make sure this happens is to establish a routine from the very beginning of the divorce process so that the child knows exactly when he will spend time with each parent.

Both of you should sit down with a calendar and show your children when they will be at each of your houses. Then get two calendars—one for each household—and mark the days "time with Mom" or "time with Dad." Put your children's activities on the calendar along with the dates when either of you will not be available, for business or personal reasons. Large calendar boards that use erasable markers work great for this family organizer. Keep one calendar at each of your houses and make sure they're up to date.

This exercise gives a child a great sense of security by knowing exactly when he will see each parent—and exactly where you are at all times. You can even write down your out-of-town phone numbers on the calendar, so your child knows how to get in touch with you. Just because you no longer live with him every day doesn't mean your child no longer has a need to know you are accessible. Also, this exercise keeps parents aware of both the child's activities and parenting time, which makes for a smoother transition from house to house for the child. If parents get into the habit of completing the calendar at the beginning of each month, it can cut down on arguments and misunderstandings over whose weekend it is or whose responsibility it is to take kids to soccer games, swim meets, Sunday school, or birthday parties. In short, it eliminates the guess work and prompts parents to regularly communicate with each other about their children.

Remember, it's the parents' responsibility, not the child's, to make sure the calendars at each home are complete. If you did this all together at the beginning of each month, and could do it without getting nasty or raising voices, your child would get the wonderful benefit of actually seeing mom and dad work together to do something for him.

"Let's Call Daddy/Mommy"

Encourage daily phone contact with the parent who is not with the child. If both parents are supportive of this, it gives a child permission to love both parents and frees her from worrying about assigning loyalty or hurting feelings. These efforts help you ensure that your child knows that having two houses doesn't mean either parent will be rejecting or creating an emotional distance—just a physical distance.

"You Promised You'd Be There!"

As you begin your life as a split family, it is very important for both parents to keep promises. If you have some doubt about whether you'll be at the soccer game, make it clear to your child beforehand. Children dealing with divorce become very sensitive to your ability to be constant and involved.

Since there is so much change right after divorce, your child has a heightened need for constancy. Provide it wherever you can. Try to keep bedtimes, mealtimes, and rules the same at both households. Resist the temptation to take the now-I'll-raise-my-children-the-way-*I*-want stance. Children of all ages may show a tendency to regress some after divorce. Thumb sucking, bed wetting, being afraid of the dark, asking for a long-ago-given-up bottle, and refusal to sleep alone are just a few of the behaviors that could arise out of your child's insecurities. Don't give in to this regressive behavior. Single moms and dads may enjoy having their empty beds filled with their children, but if you allow them to sleep with you, you are probably getting, not giving, security.

Don't fall into a pattern of being needy with your kids. Don't cry on their shoulders or turn them into your own social life. "Let's have a date!" is not an appropriate way to address spending time with your child. It implies that you don't have a date and that your child is a substitute. Another big no for parents is putting an older child into the role of coparent— "Mommy's not here, so you'll have to help me take care of your little brother and sister," or "Daddy's not here, so can I count on you to be the man of the house?" To develop normally, children should not be maneuvered into the role of caretaker for a hurting, lonely, or desperate parent.

Your child may have nightmares while he is getting used to a new house and this new split family, but don't invite him into your bed to solve the problem. New situations can be strange and uncomfortable for children, so talk about it. If your child feels unsafe in a new apartment or neighborhood, assure him that everything is going to be fine. Walk around the house and check the doors and windows together. Get a night-light, or turn on a light in the hall and leave your child's door open. Offer to sit with him while he falls asleep, and gradually shorten the length of time you stay in the room until you are back to a normal goodnight routine. If you have time to take care of a dog, get a dog and let the dog sleep in the child's room. Make sure you do whatever it takes, within reason, to keep your child feeling safe while being as independent as he should be at this developmental stage.

If you give your child two stable homes and unwavering support, the regressive behavior or nightmares will pass, and normal development will continue. If the regression or nightmares go on for more than a couple of months, or continue to get worse, get help immediately. Something is wrong, and your child is having a hard time. This behavior is a cry for help.

"But Daddy Says..."

The other nice by-product of keeping rules and routines the same at both households is that it gives children little opportunity to manipulate. It is typical for children to play one parent off against the other, testing the balance of power, or try to set up a power struggle. They do this even if divorce isn't complicating the situation. But when parents are split, the opportunities for manipulation are far greater. Parents are probably feeling guilty and may want to overindulge a child. Don't do it. Rules and routines make kids feel secure and will, over the years, prevent many problems between you and your child—and you and your ex.

"I Forgot My Soccer Uniform"

Always remember to ask your child what she would like to take from one house to the other in her overnight bag. Make sure she has whatever she needs to feel comfortable in this new place. Sometimes it's easier on everyone if certain items—toothbrushes, socks, underwear, pajamas—are duplicated because, trust me, your child will forget things, and the route between your house and your ex's house will grow longer with each trip you make.

If your child habitually forgets things and has to be taken back to her other house to pick up an item or two every time, chances are he is having trouble with the visitation schedule and is feeling homesick or parentsick. Try adjusting the schedule for shorter visitation times or encourage more phone contact. Talk to your child about what would make her more comfortable at each house; short of Daddy or Mommy moving back home, you'll probably be able to fill the requests.

I usually see this happening with the youngest children— three and under. If these children are having a hard time going back and forth, sometimes it works for the nonresidential parent to visit the child at her primary home for awhile. Then try short outings and slowly work up to a more equal division of time between the households. Again, try not to think of yourself and your need to see your child, but instead about your child's needs to feel safe and secure. Carrying a picture of Mom or Dad, or a favorite blanket, pillow, or book, really can help your child hang on to the contact with her other house.

Your child may not be forgetting items as an excuse to go see Mom or Dad again; she may just be forgetful. After all, living at two houses is complicated, and some kids are naturally more organized than others. Put together a check sheet for your child and get it laminated. Punch a hole in it and tie it to the handle of her bag. On this checklist, put all of the regular items your child needs that go back and forth— sports uniforms and shoes, homework, and so on. Make it easy on your child, and therefore yourself, and you'll avoid many trips to pick up forgotten items.

Children of divorce are easily recognizable with their bags in tow. As kids get older and used to being "bag kids" the bags will grow larger, and the items packed back and forth will multiply. They quickly learn that forgetting something causes both Mom and Dad to be angry, and so in fear of leaving anything behind, they will just pile it all in the bag.

"I Love Mommy *and* Daddy"

The variations on visitation are endless and should be customized according to the age of the children, the temperament of the children, and the dynamics of the split family. As a general rule, psychologists now believe that younger children do better with short, frequent visits from the nonresidential parent. This is due primarily to a young child's memory development. Until about the age of seven, the concept of time is incomprehensible to a child. "Next week" or "next month" as well as "for a week" or "for a month" have little or no meaning.

When divorce occurs in families with very young children, it can be a challenge for the nonresidential parent to maintain the child's sense of psychological attachment in a basic parenting relationship. Seeing a parent almost daily is very important if an infant is going to continue to recognize the parent. As an infant gets older, visits every two or three days may be sufficient to maintain recognition and further attachment. Depending upon a baby's temperament, by six months, he may be able to tolerate overnight visits.

We're treading on precarious ground here. It's very important not to disrupt the attachment to the residential parent while trying to maintain a relationship with the nonresidential parent if the child is going to feel secure and continue to develop normally. Some research has suggested that children may later develop psychological problems if attachment is disrupted at this early stage of life.

From one to three years, children begin to develop an independent sense of self. As a result, they become more aware of parental absence. This is when the type of regular schedule talked about earlier is a great help toward developing relationships with both parents. The absence of either parent during this period can cause problems later with sex-role development since this is the age when children develop their gender identity.

From three to five years old, children can tolerate more separation from each parent—up to a week is just fine in some cases. But go slow when introducing longer visitation. Some children will regress and suffer from intense separation anxiety from the parent with whom they have the stronger attachment. Also, children of this age are very susceptible to being brainwashed by one parent who is trying to alienate the other parent—a parental practice that is all too common and that can be very damaging to a child. Preschoolers have a hard time understanding that there can be good and bad in people. It's all or nothing for them, and if Mommy says Daddy is a bad guy, a child can become very confused.

From school age up until preadolescence, children can go back and forth between parents more easily, tolerating separation from each of them fairly well. However, this is the time when a child's own schedule of activities begins to interfere with parenting time. It's important for both parents to be tolerant and supportive of children's activities with sports, school, and friends in order for them to continue to develop their independence and their own sense of self.

Kids of this age will often blame themselves for any continuing problems between parents. They will try hard to "fix" the family, telling each parent they want to live with them all of the time, or anything else they think the parent wants to hear.

"I Want to Be With My Friends!"

When adolescence hits, children are trying hard to emancipate themselves from the family and to become truly independent. Making teenagers stick to a strict visitation schedule will probably end up causing a multitude of problems. Remember how busy you were as a teenager and how little time you really wanted to spend with your parents? It's only natural, and you shouldn't take it personally. Be accommodating; you'll be rewarded with a good relationship with your teen. Keep curfews and dating rules consistent between households to minimize infractions. And when your teenager screws up—which he or she probably will do—Mom and Dad need to set a reasonable punishment together and enforce it at both households to try to prevent more problems in the future.

Kids of this age often want to live with the same sex parent as they continue to learn how to be a man or a woman; they also have a tendency to want to live with the parent they saw least when they were younger. It's a last ditch effort to try to experience that relationship before adulthood. And sometimes, they'll want to be with the parent who they think will be easier to live with.

Janet, thirteen, had lived with her mother since her parents divorced when she was four. Having typical adolescent disagreements with her mother about everything from clothes and hairstyles to homework and friends, she decided she would rather live with her father and stepmother. According to her parent's divorce decree, when she was twelve, Janet had the right to choose her primary residence. Initially, looking for a little relief from being the parent of a teenager, her mother was willing to let her go live with her dad. But it wasn't long until Janet's mother, who was not remarried, was lonely and vying for Janet's return. She began to apply not-so-subtle pressure, dropping hints like "you can always change your mind." Although Janet was doing well at her Dad's, the pressure from Mom was beginning to take its toll. She began to tell some people she was happy at her dad's and others that she was miserable and wanted to go home to her mom's. After a year at Dad's, she returned to Mom's house and continues to be in a quandary. The bottom line is that whenever she feels compelled to make a choice, she hurts somebody she loves. Unless parents truly support a child in her decision about where to live, the child is put in the terrible position of rejecting a parent.

From time to time, we'll read tragic stories in the newspaper about children who have murdered a parent or committed suicide because they felt trapped in a bad situation resulting from divorce and saw no other way out. One recent case in Texas involved a beautiful, high school senior who poisoned her father because she said she couldn't figure out any other way to go back and live with her mother. Her stepfather had set a hard and fast rule for her and for his own children: no going back and forth between parents. Once she had made a decision to move in with her dad, her mother and stepfather made her stick to it. She was miserable, became depressed, and was finally so desperate and deranged that she killed her father by putting rat poison in his dinner.

Types of Visitation

Parents who fight long and hard over custody—and who are usually thinking of themselves and not their children—often end up with what I call one-week-on, one-week-off visitation. Although this type of visitation sounds equitable—and I have seen it work well when the parents live very close to one another—it can be very hard on kids. When kids spend one week in one neighborhood and the next across town, driving great distances to school and activities, they tend to have a hard time maintaining consistent friendships.

This type of arrangement can make kids into "army brats" who aren't taught early in life how to maintain solid, in-depth relationships because they've never had the opportunity to have them. Children of divorce already have a hard enough time developing relationships. If they grow up in conflict with parents who can't get along and can't provide an example of a healthy relationship, they will often steer themselves away from potential conflict by avoiding close relationships altogether. Exhausted by years of being in the middle of two warring parents, they just don't have the energy to stick with the demands of intimacy. Their attitude when conflict arises with a friend, romantic or platonic, is "I'm outta here!"

Divorced parents are often selfish with their parenting time and don't encourage children to spend time with their friends, which further reduces the number of relationship-building examples in their children's lives. Visitation becomes a control issue for parents and a platform for which to impose their style of parenting on the child during their time with them; in the worst cases, it can also be a way to punish the former spouse. This is their time to win the child over and turn the child against the other parent. Written down in black and white, it may sound stupid, but in family after family I counsel, there are parents who make these basic mistakes.

Visitation with a nonresidential parent the first, third, and fifth weekend, with dinner on a regular weeknight, is a good alternative for some families because it offers children flexibility, yet doesn't interfere with their activities during the school week. This type of schedule usually gives the nonresidential parent a chance to have the majority of summer vacation with kids, and for many children, this arrangement can work well. It is only good for the child, though, when each parent can relinquish time for the child's own special social needs and activities.

When kids don't get to see both parents during the week, they may begin to feel that one parent is no longer a part of their school and weekly routine. If you're just around for playtime, your parental relationship with your child is not fully developed. A visitation schedule that keeps both parents involved in a child's everyday life splits the week on Thursday, allowing one parent to pick the child up from school on Thursday, spend the weekend together, and then take the child to his other house on Sunday evening or to school on Monday morning. Saturdays could still be rotated in various ways to give children play time with both parents.

Another alternative is split visitation. Sometimes when there are several children in a family, one parent will be given residential custody of one child and the other parent that of another child. In these situations the visitation schedules are set so that siblings are together during "visitation" time. These are tough situations where it's hard to find solutions that please everyone. Consider the family arrangement put together for Steven, twelve, Mike, eight, and Liza, six. Steven wanted desperately to live with his father, with whom he had been most attached since a very early age, and Dad ended up with residential custody. Mom had Mike and Liza at her house. The family was able to maintain some unity because the kids were together every weekend, switching back and forth from Mom's house to Dad's house.

The middle boy, Mike, ended up having the hardest time with this arrangement. Although he was happy living with his mom, he missed his brother and was torn by wanting to be with him. Yet, he felt guilty voicing this desire or pressing his parents for change because he didn't want to leave his sister behind.

The reality is, in most divorce situations, that no perfect answer exists. It's hard for kids to find and get used to a comfort level that, at best, is less than perfect. Eventually Mike got so depressed over being away from his dad and brother that I recommended he change his primary residence to his dad's house.

"My Parents *Still* Hate Each Other"

If the anger continues to exist between parents years after divorce, children will be the ultimate losers. Austin is thirteen. His parents have been divorced for five years, but they still can't even have a telephone conversation without erupt-

ing into a screaming fight. Austin's stepfather dearly loves
him, but seeing the anger between the parents, the promises
broken by Austin's father, and the hurt it causes Austin, he
occasionally loses it, too. The result is that Austin is growing
up around three very angry adults. As a consequence his
attitude toward life in general is horrible. "Life sucks," he
says. And though he doesn't talk about suicide or threaten it, I
can't help but worry.

Austin's only outlet is Boy Scout camp, where he is away
from everyone for two wonderful weeks. The last day of camp
everyone shows up to participate in the going home cere-
monies. When it's all over, Dad says, "Come ride with me,
honey." So, Mom stands up and announces, within earshot of
all of Austin's friends and the camp counselors, "No way.
According to the decree, this is my time with Austin and I
have already given up a week for him to go to camp. He's
coming with me." Now Austin's father erupts, causing more
embarrassment and humiliation for Austin. The situation
escalates to the point that Austin shoves his father away, gets
in Mom's car, and shuts the door. He is devastated, and all the
way home, he has to hear his mother and stepfather rant and
rave about his father. Now he's mad at everyone and is already
dreading camp next year.

What do kids like Austin have to look forward to? High
school graduation—it's a nightmare. A wedding? Holidays?
Special occasions are just more opportunities for Mom and
Dad to attack one another. Kids dread these occasions, and
tend to avoid participating in anything where their parents
might be involved. The school play? Who do they go to first to
celebrate when it's over? If parents make a scene, then next
year the child just doesn't want to be involved. I had one child
who more than anything wanted to go to a particular out-of-

state school, but the idea of going to visit the school and having to deal with both parents on the trip—or heaven forbid, leave one pouting parent at home—discouraged him from even trying to get an interview. In these situations, it doesn't really matter who's at fault or what prompts the hostility; the continuing hostility and its effects on the child are the central issue.

Anger distorts thinking and keeps parents from seeing what's best for their children. Judges, sick of having to deal with hostility between parents year after year, are beginning to order counseling for divorced parents—even years after the divorce has been final. This is often used when judges see that one parent is attempting to alienate the children from the other parent. Parental alienation can take on various forms, from simple visitation interference—such as not being home when the nonresidential parent arrives to pick up the child or not informing the nonresidential parent about the child's activities—to Parental Alienation Syndrome (PAS), or even kidnapping.

PAS is visitation interference taken to the extreme where the child actually begins to refuse to see the nonresidential parent as a result of her residential parent's greater influence. A 1987 study by R. A. Gardner outlined four factors that characterize PAS: brainwashing, subtle and unconscious parental programming, factors arising within the child, and situational factors. A parent is brainwashing a child if he or she uses explicit and accusatory language about the other parent in talking to the child, saying things like "we were abandoned," or "your father cheated on us," or "your mother is a whore." Sarcasm is also an aspect of brainwashing. Comments such as "it's so sweet of your caring father to finally want to spend some time with you," or "Oh, good, she's finally spending money on you" are very damaging to a child, turning her against the nonresidential parent.[7]

More subtle comments are equally as damaging over time. A child will quickly pick up on the parent's desire for her to hate the other parent, and the child will learn not to express any desire to see the other parent or show any happiness upon seeing that parent for fear of disappointing the residential parent.

"Factors arising within the child" include the guilt over these conflicting feelings for the other parent and the fear that the residential parent will abandon him if he expresses a desire to see the nonresidential parent. Soon it's easier for the child to just join in the bashing.

"Situational factors" include witnessing a parent verbally abuse the nonresidential parent or seeing a sibling punished for enjoying the nonresidential parent so that the child supports the residential parent emotionally out of self-protection ("I don't want her to say those things to me.").

Gardner's research was based on a small population, but it indicates that the overwhelming majority of these cases in parents are females, and that 90 percent of all custody battles involve some aspects of PAS. These findings are certainly consistent with my own work. Observing one couple, ordered by the judge to go into counseling because they returned too often to court with problems they couldn't solve themselves, I fear for their children's future. The woman has become so negative and pessimistic that if the man turns his head while she is talking or shifts in his seat, she immediately erupts with a "Look at that—did you see that—he is obviously not listening to me. I don't have to take this." Her perception has become so colored against him that he has no chance to succeed in her eyes. Any and all of his behavior is interpreted by her as angry, hostile, and uncooperative. In their divorce, specific visitation times were not delineated, which gave the mother the opportunity to keep the children from going to visit their father just by saying they didn't want to go. That happened weekend after weekend until the father hadn't seen his children in months.

Though the majority of these cases are women, I have seen some fathers fall into the pattern of alienating their child's mother. Recently a six-year-old boy told me that if he asks his dad to change visitation because of an activity, the father tells him that "you're being poisoned by your mother." Putting such thoughts in the mind of a seven-year-old can cause untold psychological damage in the long term.

Because his father wants more and more time with him, he feels torn between the two major forces in his life. The child has grown fearful that he'll lose his mother, who he loves very much. "I want to tell the judge I want to live with my mom," he told me. The pressure of comments like "I miss you so much, son," "I feel sad because you're not here," or "Your mother loves your stepfather more than you" pile up on a child's shoulders and become too large a burden for him to carry.

Illustration 21: Boy, age 6, "I'm so small he can't see me"

This child's father was determined to find some way to keep him from living with his mother, who was living with another woman in a lesbian relationship. He tried to use his child as a spy, and he didn't hide his negative feelings about the mother from his son. The child, very attached to his mother and happy in the household, became terrified of leaving. As a result, he drew himself so small so that his father couldn't find him to take him away.

Illustration 21

"But, I Don't Know You..."

Another complicating factor for visitation is a mother or father who wants to reenter a child's life in a bigger way after being largely absent for a number of years. Amanda was fourteen months old when her parents were divorced. When she was four years old, her mother remarried, and they moved out of state away from Amanda's father. Now that she is ten years old, her father wants to see her more than the two or three times a year they have managed in the past.

The main problem here is that Amanda doesn't really feel close to her father, and the idea of spending every other weekend out of state and away from her friends and family, plus six weeks in the summer, is too much for her. Amanda is a bright child, she enjoys her father, but she's angry with the situation and everyone involved because she doesn't feel that she has had any control over her life. Her only chance is to try to reason with her dad and explain that having to go out of town to visit him keeps her from participating in any activities regularly, like soccer or basketball during the school year and camps or swim team in the summer. She would miss a lot of practices and half of the games or meets.

Parents don't understand that when they rigidly adhere to the court decree, they often leave their child's feelings out of the equation. Although missing a soccer game or not being able to play baseball in the summer because of visitation with an out-of-town parent may seem like no big deal right now, your child is missing an important lesson of commitment. Children who are regularly on an airplane headed out of town don't get the experience of sticking with something until it's finished, working hard for a team, or identifying with a group. All of these factors contribute to growing up healthy and happy and being successful in school. And being involved in sports can help keep kids from abusing drugs and alcohol in high school and college. So, in the end, much more is at stake than this week's soccer game.

I asked Amanda what she would do if she could design her own visitation. She said she would go to her dad's one weekend a month, have him visit her on another, and stay with him three weeks in the summer, and that would probably allow her to both see her dad and participate in the activities she wanted to do. "Right now everything is set up to his advantage, not mine," she says.

8

The New Standard of Living— "Why Can't We Afford It?"

UNLESS A FAMILY is very wealthy, divorce will negatively impact the children's standard of living. This is the economic reality. One household now becomes two; expenses double, while income usually does not. Even if a mother who hasn't worked in recent years goes back to work, she may make a good salary, but the cost of daycare will eat up a significant part of it.

"I Miss You Mommy"

When mom goes back to work, it's hard on everyone. Tempers and time are short, and kids often feel left behind as mom rushes them out the door with laptop and lunchboxes flying. Lack of time with mom was the source of extreme sadness for nine-year-old Sasha. Her mother was not only trying to maintain her professional job but was starting a business on the side—hoping to eventually be in charge of her own destiny. Sasha didn't understand the ten-year plan and only knew she missed having one-on-one time with her mom.

Suddenly, although not surprisingly, Sasha began to regress into a clinging five or six year old. She not only didn't want to grow up, she wanted to be a baby so that her mom would come back to take care of her. She needed more of her mom than her mom could give. The only solution here was for Mom to find some special time for Sasha every week, giving her something to look forward to when she felt sad. Instead Sasha's mom responded with an all-too-typical attitude. "Do you want pretty clothes? Do you want a roof over your head? Do you want me to pay the bills? Then I have to do this," was her mom's unfortunate response.

Mom going back to work can be the hardest adjustment for a child. If she is used to coming home after school to Mom, a snack and play time, then has to have a baby-sitter or stay at school for after-school care, her life totally changes. Try to explore alternatives to child care if your child has a negative reaction to it. Do you have extended family that can help out a few days? Can you share a baby-sitter with another family that has a working mom and have the kids alternate between being at your house and the other family's house?

If you need to return to the work force, look into companies that provide on-site day care so you can be close to your child and see him on a break or at lunch time. If your child is nearing the age when he could stay at home alone, carefully consider this choice. The savings may be great, but the lack of supervision could get your child in trouble. Very few kids are so self-disciplined that they will come home, get a snack, and do their homework. Most often, you'll find him sitting in front of the television waiting for you to get home. I'm not thrilled with the idea of unlimited access to television or video games, or even surfing the internet. Your child will probably be exposed to information that is too adult, and these activities can become really addictive, especially with kids ten and older.

If there are no adults at home, it's really not safe to let your kids play outside, so they're stuck in the house. If your children are enrolled in activities, and you don't have a baby-sitter to drive them, you may resort to the cab services catering to kids these days. Here you have a frightening lack of control over the people your child is associating with. I find that kids whose parents use these services on a regular basis lose enthusiasm for their activities. When your child is getting involved in an activity, whether it's soccer, ballet, gymnastics, or basketball, he wants you there to watch, to see him grow, and try and get better—not just for the match or recital. Your child will feel your lack of attachment, and soon the activity won't hold any attraction for him either.

Less Money to Go Around

As a child grows up and expenses increase, big-ticket items like private-school tuition, braces, cars, vacations, and college may be out of reach—unless parents can find a way to jointly pay for them over and above the cost of regular child support.

In most cases after a divorce, the mother's standard of living falls while the father's increases. A 1985 study of the consequences of California's no-fault divorce system, published by Lenore J. Weitzman, found a 27 percent decline in women's post-divorce standard of living and a 10 percent increase in men's. Since the majority of children still spend more residential time with their moms than their dads, the children feel the brunt of this gap.

"It's Just Not Fair"

If the lifestyle at Dad's house is easy living and the lifestyle at Mom's is scrimp and save, kids will feel guilty, to the point that they will resent Dad and won't be able to enjoy his bounty. If Mom has the money bags and Dad is scraping by, it will have the same negative effect on the kids. To children the most important issue is "what's fair." Mom and Dad are part of the same family to their child, and if one is deprived and the other is not, it's just not fair in her eyes.

In most divorce settlements, child support stops at age eighteen—with very few divorce decrees providing for the cost of college tuition. Judith S. Wallerstein and Sandra Blakeslee, in their groundbreaking book, *Second Chances: Men, Women and Children a Decade After Divorce*, found that 60 percent of the children who were eighteen years old at the time of the study, which included sixty families ten years after divorce, were on a "downward educational course compared with their fathers" and 45 percent were on "a similarly downward course compared with their mothers."[8]

Why? The mothers' incomes plus child support had not provided enough to save for college, and with fathers, the bucks stopped at age eighteen. Wallerstein and Blakeslee believe that children of divorce lower their expectations for themselves, preparing for the inevitable lack of funds for college.

"What Do You Mean We're Moving?"

While you and your ex and your divorce lawyers have been splitting up your property and liabilities, in most cases your child has been unaffected. She has been waking up in the same room and going to the same school while you've been deciding her future. The day the divorce is final, nothing's new to you—you've probably painstakingly hammered out the details. But remember, your child has been (hopefully) left out of the decision making until now. She is oblivious, living in her day-to-day life. Don't let the divorce and the changes that ensue from it be a rude awakening.

Plan your changes and let your child in on what's to come a little at a time. Don't just say one morning, "You have to start keeping your room clean because we have to put the house up for sale. And, by the way, you aren't going to go back to your school next year because we can't afford the tuition." Don't let your children come home and see a For Sale sign in the yard without warning.

Expect your child's responses to these tough changes to be very me-oriented. Expect a balk. This is an easy time to throw stones at your ex, but don't. Think of your child and the fact that you'll be doing far more damage to him than to your ex if you resort to that behavior. Instead, concentrate on dealing with the anger that should be expected from your child: "I don't want to move!" Empathize. "This isn't something I wanted either. I know these changes are hard for you, but it's the way it has to be." If both you and your ex can break the news, it's far better for your child.

It's important to understand that loss of financial status is every bit as difficult for children as it is for adults. It's helpful for children trying to get used to these changes for you to ease them into new situations slowly, one issue at a time. Introduce the most imminent change and wait to introduce the next one until it, too, is right around the corner.

If you can, don't sell the house, cut back on activities, and take your children out of private school all in the same month. Let them get used to one cutback, then introduce another until you have arrived at your new, post-divorce lifestyle.

"I Don't Want to Move"

From age six until adolescence, children grow very attached to their homes, their rooms, and their belongings. Imagine the rings produced when you throw a pebble in the water. This is how your child grows into life, "taking possession" of larger and larger areas until he is an independent adult. In the smallest ring is only mother and child, then father, siblings, and caretakers are included, then special security items like a blanket or stuffed animal, finally toys, their room, their house, the backyard, the block, the neighborhood, the school, their friends. "My house" and "my room" become important to a child's view of himself, so having to sell a house as a result of divorce can be very traumatic at this age.

There are many ways that parents can try to hang on to the family home. Sometimes child support is set to help the mother keep the children in the house. Other times fathers are given the house in the divorce settlement because their earning power and ability to pay the mortgage note is better. Still other times judges order the child to stay in the house and the parents to spend alternate weeks there with the child. This method can be disastrous for all and especially devastating financially because the parents must then maintain three households: mom's house, dad's house, and the kids' house.

"I Don't Want to Go to Another School"

Keeping your child in the same school before, during, and after divorce is worth almost any sacrifice you and your spouse can make. Making sure the school environment remains stable and constant can be a lifesaver for kids going through divorce. If they have massive change to deal with like losing their home or neighborhood or access to a parent they love and yet are allowed to hold on to this important corner of their life—they'll probably adjust better to the other changes imposed.

If you must change schools, case out the new school with your child. If there is a choice available, involve him in making the final decision. Letting a child feel that he has a choice in determining what's going to happen will make for a much more cooperative and happy participant.

Don't Just Say No

When breaking the news, do your best to be as positive as possible. Using some helpful postures and breaking the news in a positive way, you can give your child some comfort. Try to talk about changes in a "new and improved" way. Just because things are going to be different doesn't mean they are going to be worse. Don't give in to the temptation to place blame on your spouse. Kids understand the concepts of fairness and sharing. Tell your child that you and her other parent are trying to be fair to each other and are dividing what you jointly own. For instance, to be equitable, you are going to have to sell the house.

When you can't afford to buy those tennis shoes or that football jersey, don't blame it on waiting for child support or the fact that you had to pay child support even if those are the real reasons. Instead, introduce the concept of splitting the purchase price of the coveted item. Let your child do odd jobs around the house to earn her allowance. Then match her contribution to help her buy what she wants. Maybe your spouse will chip in, too, and you can split the purchase three ways. Don't, however, put your child in the middle by making her ask your ex to help pay. Before you say anything, ask your spouse to be part of the plan. If he or she won't, then don't mention it to your child.

Don't overburden your child by going into extensive explanations of your finances. Make sure that he knows you and your ex will always take care of him. Just be brief and say this year, for instance, he is only going to be able to do one after-school activity. When he asks why, don't say, "because of your father" or "because of your mother" or "because we're broke." Just say, "That's the way it has to be this year," and then let your child choose which activities to give up and which one to keep.

Don't make your child choose between activities immediately, and don't try to be chirpy offering positive alternatives your child doesn't want to hear right now, like "now we can spend more time together," or "now you can have more play time at home." Just let the disappointment sink in; your child needs a little time to process the situation. Later bring it up again, and help your child explore the positives about the change. Remember, things that may seem small to you are probably a big deal to your child. Try to say, "Just think, you won't have to put up with Jimmy on that team any more," or "Finally, we don't have to worry about clean uniforms on Thursday nights," or "Now we can watch that show that comes on when you had basketball," or "We can go sit in the stands and yell," or "You can stay up later on Fridays because you won't have games early on Saturday mornings," or "You won't have to rush so much to get your homework done," or "You can just hang out and relax."

Resist the temptation to prove to your child that you are spending all the money you can on them. I had one twelve-year-old girl tell me that her father opened up his checkbook to show her the check he had written her mother at Christmas. He wanted her to understand that he had bought the gifts under the tree. This is just not appropriate behavior.

Kids don't need to know the financial details.

The younger your child, the easier it is for her to accept the concept of giving things up. Children six and younger are more attached to people than to toys, games, homes, or activities. Chances are your only significant expenses for a young child are daycare and health care. But remember, your financial situation may be tough for a while, so start immediately instilling in your child the concept of waiting for special things like new toys or expensive tennis shoes or extravagant outings. If you've been a generous giver and that level of giving has to suddenly stop, your child will have a hard time waiting. But be patient, and she will get used to the new way of delayed gratification.

"But I Want the Jeans Tommy Has!"

Children older than six are also easily lured by "status" objects—the most popular tennis shoes, the "in" jeans. And they are more likely to be vocal and critical if parents can't supply what they feel are needed items. They aren't just being bratty if they are upset when once you could provide these things without even being asked and now you can't. You just have to get them used to the changes.

Teenagers' concerns will be predictably self-centered. Are they going to be able to have a new dress or suit for the prom? A car when they're sixteen? Can they go to the college they've chosen? Will they have to work their way through? For many post-divorce families, a car for a teenager will be out of reach. Insurance for teens is astronomical. Instead of just saying no, look hard at the budget for a car. How much could you afford to spend in your budget? Can your spouse chip in at all? What's the balance left over? Show this balance to your teenager and tell her if she can save enough to make up the difference—while still keeping grades up—then the car will happen. This method of compromise easily applies to any purchase—whether it's tennis shoes, a bicycle, or anything your child truly needs or pines for.

Parents need to resist the temptation to send children with special requests to the nonresidential parent. I find this often happens over summer expenses like camp. Out of anger the ex who has been the primary breadwinner makes a statement to the other parent that he or she's not paying for camp tuition this summer. So the breadwinner parent tells the child they'll have to ask the other parent to pay for it. I've had parents tell their child to "write a letter to your Dad" or to "ask Mom real nicely," and then maybe they'd get to go to camp. Children will quickly pick up on these manipulative behaviors and learn how to be resourceful to get what they need—a lesson I don't think they need to learn when they are six, seven, or eight.

One seven-year-old boy told me he just let his shoes hurt his toes rather than telling Mom or Dad he needed new ones. If he asked his mom, she would tell him to ask his dad because he made more money than she did. If he asked his dad, he would get mad because his mom hadn't already taken care of it. What did she use his child support money for anyway?

Time Out to Think

Parents are so overwhelmed with the massive change divorce brings to their own lives that they often overlook how these changes affect their children. Take some time out to think. Sit on your child's bed one day while she is out. Look around the room and try to imagine yourself in her place. Think about the changes from your child's perspective. On another day, walk your neighborhood and take your child's favorite route to friends' houses. Or sit in the park or the school parking lot and get into your child's thought process. How will divorce affect her?

Try to see the world and the changes you're immersed in through your child's eyes. What are your child's needs? How can you meet those in a pared-down way? Don't degrade your child because her priorities seem superficial to you. Kids, especially adolescents, are very self-oriented and self-conscious.

Maybe you can keep the clothing labels your child has come to love by shopping differently, during sales or at outlet malls. Maybe your child can still play soccer if you find a school with a soccer team that's not as expensive as the club soccer he plays. Maybe your child can't swim at the country club because you have to give up a membership, but he can join the YMCA and keep on swimming.

If you find yourself saying "no" and "we can't" all of the time instead of finding creative ways around the negatives, it will only add to the depression your child is already feeling about the divorce. Try to find second bests to replace what was. Get your child used to the idea of not always getting his first choice, but getting a second or third choice instead. This is a great lesson for life, because none of us gets what we want every time.

9

Moving Day—"Do We Have To Move?"

WHILE DIVORCE is traumatic, moving is stressful and upsetting too, especially for a child who is leaving what may have been the only sources of stability in his life—school and friends. By following some simple guidelines that will help you consider the move from your child's perspective as well as involve him in the decision-making process, you can make the introduction of a new home, neighborhood, friends, and school as painless as possible.

Depending upon your child's temperament and age, moving can be either fun or a nightmare. Some kids embrace new things, people, and situations, and if they are involved in the moving process, they will jump right in. Other kids, who are afraid of newness and change and the uncertainty that comes with it, will be terrified. The advice in this chapter applies to all children, but you may use more or less of it depending upon your child's unique personality. The main point, however, is that you need to consider your child's needs and not just your own in the impending move.

Take things slowly if you can. Most divorces drag on. Selling a house will take time. Try putting your house on the market a few months before school is out, hoping that a move will take place in the summer. Prepare your child for this event. Don't let him come home and find a For Sale sign in the yard. Discuss the fact that you and your ex are dividing things up in a way that is fair to you both, and the house has to be sold so you can do that.

If you can stay in the same school system, the move will be much easier on your child. If that's not a possibility, do some exploring and narrow your choices of neighborhoods by schools. Take your school-age child with you when you go tour a potential new school, and consider his input as you narrow the choices. Make sure he understands that the final decision is yours, but that you are interested in his wishes and will consider what he thinks is important, too. You may also need a new day-care provider when you move, so enter that into the equation. Then pick a realtor or apartment selector service that specializes in the neighborhoods you've chosen.

Make looking for a new house or apartment a family project. Sit down with your kids and discuss everyone's needs, likes, and dislikes. You may be downsizing, but that doesn't mean you can't find something for everyone to look forward to in the move. Maybe a child that has shared a bedroom will get his own. Maybe you'll find a fenced backyard or a house with a playroom. Maybe the new house is more conducive to a pet. Maybe you'll find an apartment complex that has a playground and a pool. Maybe it's a neighborhood with more kids the age of your children. Or maybe your house or apartment will be near a big park.

If both you and your spouse are going to be looking for new

places to live, consider looking in the same neighborhood. The same street and the same block are probably too close and will be uncomfortable for all. But if you and your ex are just a few blocks away from each other, it can be a great time-saver for you while providing needed continuity for your children. This is the type of arrangement that works well only for parents with joint custody who have been able to stay congenial.

When you've defined all these desires, make a wish list and share it with your realtor or take it along when you go look at apartments.

"But Who Will Be My Friends?"

Finding a neighborhood with children the age of yours is one of the best things you can do for your child right now. You are providing your child with a built-in support group to help her get through the next tough year of life. Of course, there's no guarantee she will like the other kids in the neighborhood or vice versa, but at least you are making sure she has choices.

If you don't provide these opportunities, you truly limit your child's development. Spending too much time with you at an age when she should be spending more time with peers will almost always add to the sadness or depression that results from a divorce. Chances are your child won't be happy with you or your ex, and she won't feel at home in either house. Around adolescence, kids experiencing this kind of anomie express the desire to go away to boarding school. This isn't necessarily a bad alternative for an older child having a hard time adjusting to a move or divorce. It allows her to be in a peer environment, escape the pain of divorce, and put together a life of her own.

"Where's the Ice Cream Store?"

As moving day nears, make your new neighborhood as

familiar and kid-friendly as possible. Play detective and walk around getting familiar with everything. Find the cleaners you'll use, the grocery store, the nearest place for ice cream or frozen yogurt. Find the fastest route to school and let your child time it. Plan a weekend bicycle outing in the new neighborhood. Find the safest way to get to the park or the lake or the bike trail. Is there a YMCA or a community center nearby? If you find one, check it out. Explore. Make it fun.

If your child is a baby-sitter, help her start networking. Make a flier and go meet your neighbors. Check out the Parents Day Out program at a neighborhood church, synagogue, or community center. Introduce your child to the teachers, and see if they have a bulletin board for baby-sitters where she can post her name and phone number. This is a great way to learn the ages of the neighborhood kids and meet other parents. You also may find daycare alternatives for your littler ones in the process. Does the neighborhood have a baby-sitting co-op or a mother's forum that meets regularly?

Find out if the neighborhood has an association and, if it does, join it. Does it publish a newsletter? If so, see if the newsletter has a place where new families are introduced to the neighborhood. Is there a block party coming up you could attend with your child?

Keep It Safe

Unfortunately it's necessary to have a safety conversation with each of your children when you move into a new neighborhood. Do this with each child separately because different rules will apply to different ages, and you want your conversations to be age appropriate. Set new safety boundaries for the new house and go over them with your child carefully. Don't get preachy or repetitive. Once is usually

enough with an occasional positive reminder. ("It's really
great that you remembered to lock the door when you came in
from playing. Thanks.") If you act too concerned, or if you
send out constant reminders in a negative way, you risk
making your kids paranoid. ("I thought I told you to lock the
door—do you know how dangerous that is?")

The "stranger danger" issue is a touchy one, with the
important question being how much do you stress? If you talk
about *all* of the danger out there in explicit terms, are you
protecting your children or scaring them? My philosophy is of
the less-is-more school. Make sure your kids are comfortable
talking with you—about anything. Set parameters for them
that you feel are safe. Avoid putting them in risky situations.
Then make sure they know they can tell you everything, any
time. Try a blanket invitation such as, "If anyone ever makes
you feel uncomfortable, then just tell me about it."

Moving Day

Moving day is hectic, so plan ahead so that your children don't
get lost in the process. Let them help. Give everyone a job.
Kids of almost any age can pack their favorite things. Give
them a box and let them fill it up and label it. Make these the
last ones on and the first ones off the truck, so when you get
to the new house, they know exactly where their favorite
things are and can get them settled.

Change is ruling your life right now, but chances are your
children feel more out of control than you do. Let them have
some control. If you give them leeway in setting up their own
rooms, there will be far less anger directed at you even though
the move is still causing some hard feelings. If kids are going
to have to share a room and they haven't before, help set up
some boundaries for "private" areas within the room. An-

other helpful rule is to give each child a certain amount of time alone in the room.

Sam and Dan, ten, and twelve, had to share a room for the first time after their parents divorced. The biggest source of argument was who got to sleep in the top bunk. The solution was simply to alternate. Certain privileges also went with the top or bottom bunk. The boy in the top bunk had to get dressed for bed in the bedroom, the boy in the bottom bunk in the bathroom. The one in the bottom bunk turned out the lights. Also, each boy got an hour a day alone when the room was off-limits to the other one.

During a Divorce, Kids Also Feel Confused and Out of Control

Illustration 22: Boy, age 8
Divorce is confusing to kids. In this child's family there were two new homes, a new school, and new "friends" in Mom's and Dad's life. All of this newness made this child feel out of control.

Illustration 23: Boy, age 10
Divorce is about change, and change can be confusing. This little boy said he never knew which end was up. When his father left the house, routine did too, leaving him exasperated.

New Place, New Rules

Moving day gives you a great opportunity to redefine how your family works together in making the house run. You're a single parent now and have less time and fewer hands to get the job done at home. So, enlist some help from your children. If they haven't had chores before, find some for your kids to

Illustration 22

Illustration 23

do. Even a toddler can learn to put his own toys away.

Ask your children to start fixing their own school lunches—and maybe one for you, too. Make dinner a real family affair where everyone has a job. Your kids will enjoy helping you plan the menus, shop, and chop. Cook together on weekends, making weekday meals ahead of time. Pick a night when each child is boss in the kitchen. Make one night pizza night and designate another evening to eat out. Dinner can become something everyone does together.

"I Don't Want to Go to School"

You've laid good groundwork, then the first day of school arrives, and you are in a tug of war to get out the door. Ease your child into the new situation just as you did on her first day of preschool or kindergarten. If you were able to move in the summer, get your child familiar with the school by using the playground, walking the grounds, and taking the route to school together. When school opens, go with your child to meet the principal and his teachers. Walk the halls together. Get a tour of the campus, the library, the auditorium, the gym. For some really sensitive kids, that may be enough for the first day. The next day, maybe you can walk your child to class and go meet him for lunch. The next day walking to the door of the school may be enough. Wean your child gradually until he is more independent.

If your child is still having difficulty adjusting, set a designated time for him to go to the school office and call you at home or work for some extra reassurance. Use positive reinforcement to help your child start to relax in the new situation. Try saying, "I bet you're really proud of yourself that you've made it so far today. That's great!" or "Weren't you so proud that you went right to your class this morning!"

For children in day care, regressing into some separation anxiety is also common. If you can, go be with your child at lunch for the first week. Or ask your employer if you can leave work early for the first week. The next week, try every other day. Maintaining some extra physical contact with little ones during this transition time is helpful.

"I Miss My Old Friends"

Your child will be missing a lot of things right now including the way things were when Mom and Dad were married, the nonresidential parent, and the familiarity of the old house, school, and neighborhood. Maintaining ties with previous friends can help your child deal with the change and strangeness of her new life. Have old friends over to spend the night or involve them in weekend activities. If your child is old enough to have phone time, get a list of phone numbers so she can keep in touch.

College Kids

When there's less to go around after a divorce and mom or dad is searching for a way to make ends meet through a move, often the child who has gone to college will come home and find that he no longer has a room at home. This can be really upsetting and scary to a kid who is one step away from independence. I've seen these situations force girls and boys into stronger attachments with their girlfriends and boy-friends as they search for some stability and a place to call home.

It's important to make sure your college-age child has a special place in your new home. Whether it's a place to store stuff that doesn't go to college, a nook in a guest room, a corner of a sibling's room, or a room of their own, they need a presence in the house. Again, if you involve your son or daughter in the decision, they'll see the necessity of not taking up a whole room in a house at the expense of crowded siblings; after all, they'll only be there a few nights and summers. Broach the problem and let them help you arrive at a logical solution. Then they'll know you didn't just push them out of the nest. Don't worry, they're almost ready to go.

Julie is a freshman in college who was shocked with the unhappy news that her parents were divorcing, selling their house, and moving out of the suburb where she had grown up and gone to high school. Though she was living a fairly independent life as a college student, the thought of not having something familiar to come home to was devastating, forcing Julie into an unhealthy attachment with her boyfriend that was based on dependence and the need for something familiar. Julie felt that she no longer had a home base. She was just "out there."

My advice to Julie's parents was, "slow down." If they could just wait a year to make these changes, Julie would probably be ready for them. So often kids only come home from college that first summer, anyway. After that, they are ready to stay at college for summer school or work an internship or, if the funds are there, travel.

Moving Away

This is among the most volatile issues of divorce. It's hard enough for children to move apart from one parent or to go back and forth between houses in the same city or town, but when one parent moves away to another city or state, it can produce much added stress.

We live in a very transient and mobile society, and when one parent needs to relocate, it's usually for a job. I try to encourage parents to avoid this tough situation at all costs. If you can stay in the same city—even if you'll be making less money—do it. If not, approach moving out-of-town in much the same way you approach moving across town, by involving your children step by step.

Even if your children will be spending very little time in the home of the parent who is moving away, it is important for them to have their own space there. Expect reactions to moving or visiting the parent who has moved away to be exaggerated compared to just moving into a new home in the same town. Your children will probably experience separation anxiety from all that was familiar—family, home, neighborhood, school—and will be reluctant to embrace the new. Progress slowly and show a lot of love along the way. If you are the parent who must move away from your children, try to see them at least once a month—more often for children under school age. Because of the distance between you, prepare yourself for being less of a priority to your children. Distance will test your bonds.

Acknowledge how difficult this is for them and talk about it. Tell them how proud you are of them for being brave through these hard times. Make sure they know that both parents—even though you live far apart—are always going to take care of them. Large long-distance phone bills are a small price to pay for the well-being of your children. Encourage frequent phone contact with the parent who has moved away, daily for the younger kids.

If phone calls become too tear filled and disruptive at bedtime, try having your children call when they come home from school each day. Mornings are usually hectic, but a predinner phone call with Mom or Dad can ease your children's fears.

There are situations in which a move away from a parent

may actually help the children, particularly when the animosity between parents is out of control or when one parent has elected to be absent a lot from his or her children's lives. Some parents aren't ready for the responsibility of children and respond by not being active in their care. Others are suddenly single and forget that they are parents. Whatever the reason for the absence, it hurts the children. If that absent parent moves away, or if the children and the residential parent move away, children can better deal with this lack of attention.

After a number of years away from their children, some absentee parents will become resentful, most often over child support, and seek more frequent visitation. This can be a very painful and frightening time for children, who quickly pick up on their absentee parent's resentment. In the families where I've been involved, children see through parents' attempts to appear sincere; they understand the real reasons for the new visitation schedule: their parents want to "get something" in return for the child support, or are trying to punish the ex.

If an absentee parent really wants to have a closer relationship with his or her children, he or she should first try it on the kid's turf. If you visit your children more often, respecting their routines and activities and building your relationships slowly, your children will eventually feel more comfortable coming to you.

10

The Future —"Will We Always Be a Family?"

AFTER A DIVORCE, one of the best things you can do is try to restore stability in your child's life and create a new sense of family. Invent new routines and new traditions at holidays and special occasions. Show your child that "new" doesn't have to mean "not as good as it used to be."

If you can, work with your ex-spouse to set up similar rules and routines in both houses, which will give your child a feeling of continuity and comfort. This is difficult when one parent spends only weekends with the kids and they don't have to get up for school and follow the workday routines. But bedtime, mealtime, bath time, and study time should be standardized to help your child feel comfortable in both homes. Also, make sure he has similar, age-appropriate responsibilities at both households so that one parent isn't seen as easy and the other one as the enforcer. (Try to avoid giving your child adult jobs that used to be handled by your spouse—for example, asking the oldest to care for youngest, thus putting him in the role of the absent mother or father.)

Jason, a ten-year-old boy, who lives primarily with his father, had trouble getting schoolwork done at his mother's house. Instead of telling his mother that he had to study, he would go along with whatever activities she had planned, afraid he would hurt her feelings. Then when he did poorly on tests, he'd get in trouble with his dad. This situation could have been prevented if there had been a set study time at mom's house just as there was at Dad's.

Parents often don't understand that rules and boundaries are part of what makes children feel safe, loved, and in control. Each parent should be responsible for enforcing rules at his or her own house. If the father had been the disciplinarian when they lived together as a couple, the mother can't expect him to continue that role at her house by making threats to call Daddy or by asking him to talk to the children about discipline problems at her home. Both parents should take part in setting guidelines and consequences when children don't follow them. This doesn't mean you have to march around your house like a dictator. Rewarding good behavior is the best way to teach your children to obey the rules.

Once you have established post-divorce living arrangements, don't bring up the question of change in an effort to make your child happy. If your child wants a change, she will ask you about it. Otherwise, let her settle in to the newly established routine. Now your child's family is essentially two separate families—one at Dad's house, the other at Mom's. The more those two homes are alike, the less confusion for your child.

Letting Go of Anger

I've said it before, but it's worth repeating: divorced parents need to make every effort to get along and be civil to each other. It's a confusing relationship for your child because he loves you both, but you don't love one another. But if you can at least learn to like each other, it will ease your child's anxiety and help him accept this new family format. It's good for your child to see you and your ex doing things together for him, but only if you can do it without arguing. If your child is going to have to start a new school, take him to school together. Both of you should plan to meet teachers or attend PTA meetings. You should also both try to attend soccer games, recitals, and other activities. Now that your divorce is final, sit together, if you can do it without showing animosity, so that your child doesn't have to choose who to run to when the event is over and it's time for kudos. I've had kids tell me that when they went to the parent closest to the stage or the soccer field, the other parent would leave in a huff. Try to put your own feelings aside and focus on celebrating your child together.

I know these situations and the feelings evoked, are complicated, but divorce does complicate your life and your child's life. You'll have some challenges to overcome no matter how hard you work for peace.

If there was major conflict during your divorce that you've been vocal about, your children will have a tendency to take sides. The best thing you can do to discourage this reaction is to henceforth refrain from criticizing your ex-spouse in front of your child. Parents need to make divorce final for their child; they need to resist showing anger over the habits and traits they didn't like about each other during the marriage. Although you may feel you have reason to let off steam, you are only creating conflict within your child, conflict that will cause problems in her life now as she gets used to two families and later when she begins to have relationships of her own.

A daughter growing up in a household where the mother complains about the father, for instance, will often marry someone who is frighteningly similar to the man who is the subject of her mother's complaints. The underlying psychological dynamic is that Dad has rejected mother and daughter, so if the daughter can grow up and marry someone similar to Dad and make him love her, then maybe Dad really loved her, too.

Divorced parents need to realize that they will be parents to their children for the rest of their children's lives. Decisions about health care and education will be ongoing. The sooner parents find a way to work together, the better it will be for their children.

"Why Don't You Like Mommy/Daddy?"

As an expert witness in many divorce proceedings, I have seen more horror stories than I care to relate on these pages. The damage to children is incalculable. At the root of each tragedy is at least one parent who has forgotten his responsibility to his child and is caught up in winning a battle. If you imagine all of our emotions as being on a key ring, love and hate are right next to each other. When parents' love for each other turns to hate, their anger can make them forget about the welfare of their child.

If you can't stop experiencing surges of rage even after your divorce is final, get some help. You're no good for your child if you're consumed by anger over a failed relationship. When you are healthy again, you'll be able to make your child the priority. If you haven't let go of your anger, your children may be more aware of it than you are—as the following illustrations show very clearly.

Illustration 24: Girl, age 10
While this little girl's father has remarried and had

Illustration 24

another child, her mother has gone from one failed relationship to another, eventually blaming each of them on the child's father. Divorce can become the ubiquitous excuse for some parents, a practice that gets old fast for kids.

Illustrations 25 and 26: Girl, age 13
    This illustration and the one below were drawn by a child who got over her parents' divorce long before her mother did.

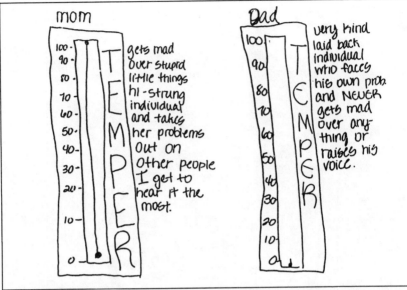

Illustration 25

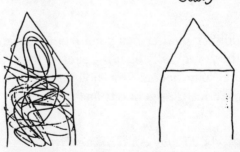

= Yelling, fighting, and negativity.

My mom gets angry with me over little things like you didn't turn off the T.V., Because I woke you up late and you missed your bus your grounded for a week from the phone.

moms   Dads

Illustration 26

Children do have the ability to go on with their lives, as this little girl did, but often parents, like this child's mother, remain depressed and dejected year after year and eventually drag their children down with them.

"I Just Want to Be Normal"

The kids I see tell me they just want to be normal. If visitation is truly that—just a visit with their other parent—the parent will often plan a weekend full of activities to make sure the child has fun. Sometimes this is a thinly veiled effort to try to win allegiance. Other times it's the result of a parent who is uncomfortable spending time with his or her child and has to plan every minute out of fear of simple downtime.

Most kids, however, would just rather be at home playing with other kids, by themselves, or spending time with you. Children of divorce often miss out on what they call "the normal stuff" because parents can't communicate or make plans without first consulting their children. So, children of divorced parents miss the birthday parties and the slumber parties and getting to accept invitations from friends because "that's my time with Dad/Mom."

Kids want to fit in. They don't want their friends or their teachers to know that there's anything different about them. That's why they'll want to change their last name if their mom remarries. That's why they'll want to call their stepmother "Mom" in front of their friends. They want to feel that they have a normal family.

Taylor, eight, likes his Dad's girlfriend and started calling her "Mom" even though she and his dad have only been dating six months, and there is no talk of marriage or even engagement. She wasn't a replacement for his real mother. Austin just felt a strong need to have a whole family—even if it was just for the weekend. The first time he went back to his mom's, he told her all about Dad's neat girlfriend and the great time they had. When he saw his mom's reaction, he felt that he had hurt her feelings, so now he feels uncomfortable talking about anything with her. He is so afraid he is going to say something wrong, he simply shut down.

Unfortunately adults get defensive and possessive instead of diagnostic. When your child says in a fit of anger, "I don't want you to be my daddy anymore!" don't jump to conclusions that your ex-wife has been baiting him to say this. It's normal for children to say things like this to their parents when they're mad. Would you freak out about this outburst if you weren't divorced? Probably not. Instead, you would try to figure out what was bothering your child—it's probably something pretty obvious—let things settle down, and then talk about it.

When divorce is a factor, your ability to diagnose needs to get a bit more sophisticated. Still, don't overreact if your child blurts out something hurtful—unless this behavior becomes the rule instead of the exception. If your relationship with your child is truly suffering, then you have to figure out why. Ask yourself some questions. Is your child being discouraged from having a relationship with both parents? Is the other parent implying he or she is miserable when your child is with you, making your child feel guilty about being away? If you are remarried, does your child feel that he needs to stay with your ex and take care of him or her because he or she is alone? Re-examine your own behavior. Does your child feel left out of your new family? Is the birth of a new baby taking away attention from your older child?

Are you spending time with your child or is the television

and a sack full of candy and videos your routine? You don't have to go to Disney World; just take a walk together or ride bikes or play catch or cards, go to the pool, give the dog a bath, plant some flowers.

Someone to Talk to

"Don't Make Me Go to Mommy's/Daddy's"

If your child begins to refuse to go to the other parent's house, it is cause for concern—and should be cause for concern to both parents. Bring in an outside professional to monitor the situation. This professional will be able to judge what's happening and what kind of interaction is going on with one or both parents that could be causing this reaction. Abuse is a possibility; so is parental alienation. Is your child having other problems? Sleep disturbance, bedwetting, loss of appetite, a sudden drop of grades in school are all areas to explore. Be sure you pass on information to the professional to help you get to the source of the problem as quickly as possible.

Your behavior toward your ex will have a profound effect on the child. One boy, who saw his father only under supervised visits, would spend that time standing and facing the wall with his back to his dad. After a little investigation, the counselor found that the mother and stepfather hated the father passionately and, since they didn't mask their disdain in front of the child, they had made the child feel he was not allowed to play with his father. He was terrified—not of his father but of his mother and stepfather being upset with him if he had fun.

If your child is having a particularly difficult time adjusting to your divorce, try looking for support groups in your area. One that has many chapters is called the Banana Split Club. Most often groups like these are offered through your child's school. This setting gives your child the opportunity to talk about complaints and concerns with other children whose parents are divorcing. It's a comfort for your child just to know that what he or she is feeling isn't strange and that other kids are having the same problems.

Your child has lots of new challenges to work through, and a group counseling situation can help. Kids in divorced families have to find a whole new way to relate to their parents; for instance, they no longer have Mom or Dad to act as an intermediary for them. They can no longer beg, "Mom, will you ask Dad for me?" Suddenly a child is forced to deal one-on-one with each parent.

Even when your child seems to have adjusted to the divorce, anxieties can arise years later. Looking for colleges, your child may have a recurrence of old worries when he has to choose which parent will take him on those trips. Both parents may be paying for college, so someone's feelings will be hurt if both aren't included. Even later at weddings, deciding who sits where can be a nightmare. Do your best to ease those anxieties for your child by keeping critical comments about your ex to yourself and letting your child know you don't want him to worry over the details of your personal life.

I had a patient, a senior in high school, who finally made himself physically sick at the prospect of having to go visit colleges with both of his parents. After having been divorced for years, they still couldn't get along. Severe anxiety brought on a case of mononucleosis that eventually prevented the trip. Later these anxieties would emerge at parents' day, graduation—and anytime this boy had to be together with both of his parents.

"I Want to Move in With Mom/Dad"

If you get residential custody of your child, and she sees your ex primarily on weekends, prepare yourself for the time when she will want to move in with your ex. Most often this will happen around age twelve or thirteen. Sometimes kids want to live with the "easier" parent, which is another reason I encourage parents to have the same rules at both houses. Other times the child chooses to live with the same-sex parent, who will serve as a role model during adolescence. But more often, children have a need to be parented by both parents. It's hard on you, the parent who is left at home, to get a taste of what your ex has dealt with for years, but it's something you have to let happen.

Children don't necessarily know what's best for them at this age, but if a child feels that she didn't get to see enough of her other parent, she will want to try it out. Let her. Give it a trial run or, at the very least, work for a compromise.

"Mommy Has a Boyfriend"

When divorced parents begin to move on with their lives and form new relationships, children can develop fresh insecurities and anxieties. Not only does this destroy your child's hopes that you will reunite with the other parent, but it also can set him up for disappointment if your new relationship doesn't work out. Until you feel that your new boyfriend or girlfriend may become permanent, it's best to keep these adult activities separate from your time with your child. He has already experienced a great loss, so if there's any chance that you may have another failed relationship, save him from going through the process again. Don't let your child get attached to someone who may just be a brief interlude.

I often talk with children whose parents have introduced them to their friend of the opposite sex and who have insisted, "We are just friends." Trust me, your children know whether someone is just your friend or not. They are very intuitive and often far wiser than you imagine.

When you feel it's time to introduce your child to your new significant other, do it gradually in short sessions. Meet for a meal. Don't push it by planning a whole afternoon or evening together. And don't try to give your friend time alone with your child in the beginning. This won't help them get to know each other faster, it will only make your child uncomfortable.

Be prepared for your child to fear that this new person will steal away your affections. For this reason, don't be openly affectionate toward your friend in the early stages of this introduction. Wait until your child is secure in the belief that your having a relationship with someone doesn't change your feelings for him.

If you push a relationship between your child and your new friend, your child may begin to misbehave or act like a baby to test his ability to get your complete attention. Remember, he may be embarrassed by your relationship as well as resentful and anxious. A common new complaint would be, "I hate it here and I want to go live with Dad/Mom." If this happens, go back a few steps and start again more slowly after your child has had some time to regain a sense of security.

Of course it's best for divorced parents to go on with their lives, but it can also cause their children to be anxious, to act out, or to withdraw and become depressed. I had one nine-year-old patient who was brought to my office because he had said he wanted to die. His ultimate problem was that he had lost his position in the family. Both of his parents were remarried, and they both had new babies. He was confused and had developed an extreme case of separation anxiety. His parents were so focused on their new relationships that neither one had noticed his withdrawal until it became serious.

Stepparenting

Thanks in large part to the story of Cinderella and similar narratives and myths, stepparenting has gotten a very bad name. Stepmothers are ugly and mean, stepfathers are suspect, and stepchildren are not really a part of the family. It doesn't have to be this way if the stepparent and parent exercise some patience and understanding.

The most important factor contributing to good stepparenting relationships is a decent relationship between the stepparent and the ex-husband or ex-wife. Stepparents, just like parents, need to keep any negative feelings about their stepchild's other parent to themselves—no innuendoes, no snide remarks, no negative body language. If a stepparent wants to have a good relationship with his or her stepchild, he or she needs to always keep in mind that the other parent is someone this child loves. When you say hurtful things about that parent, you're hurting the child, too, and forcing her to take sides.

If the parents still fight, the stepparent needs to stay out of it. If the stepparent does this well, he or she will become a neutral zone for the child—somewhere safe and nonjudgmental for the child to go when she is upset by Mom and Dad. This can be a saving grace for a child whose parents stay at each other's throats year after year. At least there is one adult in this child's life who doesn't seem angry and suspicious all of the time.

The best way to approach stepparenting is to start out

simply by being friends with the child while still dating the child's parent. Go slowly and don't push. Let the child take the lead. If the stepparent also has children, don't force the children together. It's great to try activities that all of the children will enjoy together, but don't expect fast friendships to develop. Make sure they have plenty of opportunity to get to know one another before marriage is discussed.

As the relationship develops, a stepparent will naturally move into more of a parenting role from one of friendship. With parenting comes discipline, which can be a sensitive area for the stepparent. The child—and the child's parent—will probably be taken aback the first time a stepparent moves into the role of disciplinarian. "You aren't the boss of me," would be a typical reaction from a small child, who will immediately turn to his parent for backup. The best way to handle this scenario is to talk about it before a disciplinary problem arises. Make sure parent, stepparent, and child are all aware of the house rules and the consequences of breaking them. Put these rules and consequences on paper and post them on the refrigerator. Explain to the child that the step-parent has equal authority with the parent. And if a step-parent and parent disagree about the child's behavior or about punishment, discuss it out of earshot and present your decision as a unified team.

If a parent and stepparent have a child together or if the stepparent's children live in the household and the stepchild does not, it's only natural for the stepchild to feel left out. I recently had a child tell me that his dad was taking his stepmother and her children on a cruise. The boy couldn't go because it wasn't his time with his dad. I tell parents to try to avoid these situations if possible. It sends a message of rejection to the child and makes him feel "second class," as if he doesn't really belong to either family.

If you do develop a close relationship with a stepchild, remember to keep adult issues to yourself. I had one little girl tell me that she had been worried and upset because her stepmother had told her she and the girl's father weren't going to pay for her brother's school tuition any longer. The little girl's mother didn't know this yet, and the child was overburdened by the secret.

Getting a Grip

I've seen parents and children do the most incredible things. There was the seven year old, for instance, who told me he gets mad at his dad because the dad records everything he says. Why? "I guess to give it to his lawyer," responded the child. There was a father who got custody of a two year old he barely knew just to hurt his ex-wife, then entrusted this baby to the care of an alcoholic girlfriend. Or the father who makes his nine year old put the child support check in the envelope to mail to his mother to make sure the child knows how much money is paid to her each month. I know a sensitive child who hides in the bushes when his father comes to get him because he doesn't fit in with his more aggressive father and half brothers. There is also the child who has come to hate her father so much for hating her mother year after year that she legally changed her name to her mother's maiden name.

Even older children continue to suffer from their parents' insensitivity. I know a twenty-three year old who can't have a serious relationship with a woman because he is still afraid to care. He learned the lesson very young that caring hurts.

Or there is the thirty-seven year old who won't invite both her mother and her father to her wedding for fear they'll make a scene, so she invites neither.

Children can come through divorce in spite of their

parents' difficulties and grow up to be healthy adults capable
of lasting relationships. But it won't be easy. Why should you
make them work so hard? Isn't that what parenting is all
about—giving your children the tools and knowledge to make
their lives easier or better than yours?

When I ask children of divorced parents how they would
avoid divorce themselves, too often they say they wouldn't get
married in the first place. But sometimes their answers are
wise beyond their years: "I wouldn't rush into anything," says
an eleven-year-old girl. "I would always work for a compromise," says a ten-year-old boy.

Listen and learn is what I tell parents, meaning, listen *to
your children*. You will learn from them.

Appendix I

The Questionnaire—Children on Divorce

I used the following questionnaire to give children the opportunity to be heard about how divorce has changed their lives. The answers to these questions are in their own words. By listening to them, we can learn how to help many other kids survive divorce.

The Questions

What divorce does to you is really important to me. I want to know how certain problems have made you feel. Please tell me what happened to you in the following situations.

1. How did you feel when your parents began to argue or when you began to notice that your parents were not happy?

2. How did your parents tell you what was going to happen?

3. How did you first feel about what was happening, when things started changing like your dad or mom stopped coming home or began coming home very late, or when one of your parents moved out?

4. What did your parents tell you about what was going to happen? How did they tell you?

5. What changes happened? Did you have to move, or did everything stay the same?

6. How did your parents change? How did they start acting around you?

7. How do you wish they would have handled the situation?

8. What was it like going to visit your dad or mom for the first time?

9. How do you feel about the times to visit? What is it like going back and forth? What if you forget something at the other house?

10. How has the divorce changed your life?

11. How have your parents changed toward you? Are they acting different from when they were living in the same house?

12. What else can you tell me about how you feel?

13. What do you wish could be different?

14. Do you think it's a good idea for kids twelve years old or older to have the power to choose whom to live with?

Girl, Age 16
Age at Time of Divorce: 14

1. How did you feel when your parents began to argue or when you began to notice that your parents were not happy?
I didn't know what to do. There were a lot of fights over us, over me. I thought I was the problem because I was the center of the fights, the ones I heard.

2. How did your parents tell you what was going to happen?

My dad just left for the second time.

3. How did you first feel about what was happening, when things started changing and your dad or mom stopped coming home or began coming home very late, or when one of your parents moved out?

Mad, angry, sad, mixed, relieved, stressed.

4. What did your parents tell you about what was going to happen? How did they tell you?

My mother was not very honest toward me. She kept it kind of secretive for a while. I would have rather have known from the beginning.

5. What changes happened? Did you have to move, or did everything stay the same?

It was really stressful and felt abnormal. I didn't have freedom to do what I wanted to do any more. I was really mad at first because I had to take on more responsibilities because I'm older.

6. How did your parents change? How did they start acting around you?

My father was nice at first, actually real cool. Then some days he was nice and some days he would bite my head off. My parents talked bad about one another, but my dad didn't try to buy me like you would think.

7. How do you wish they would have handled the situation?

More maturely. I wish my mom wouldn't hang up on him. My dad doesn't do that. He brought papers for her to sign. She wouldn't sign, and so he got mad and left. His temper is worse.

8. What was it like going to visit your dad or mom for the first time?

I never went in eight months. I avoided it because I didn't want to see where his new life is.

9. How do you feel about the times to visit? What is it like going back and forth? What if you forget something at the other house?

Child did not answer.

10. How has the divorce changed your life?

It takes a lot more to earn my trust now. I don't have as much support as before. I have to be more responsible for my brothers and sisters. Now whatever Mom says goes. I used to have one parent see my point.

11. How have your parents changed toward you? Are they acting different from when they were living in the same house?

They get angry easier and are making all kinds of new rules. They treat me something like a maid or nanny.

12. What else can you tell me about how you feel?

Confused. I get annoyed talking about the whole thing. Kind of scared. It messed it up with my boyfriend. He had the perfect family. Only friends whose parents are divorced understand me. I don't have to say a word—they just know.

13. What do you wish could be different?

I wish I had a happy family and a honest father.

14. Do you think it's a good idea for kids twelve years old or older to have the power to choose whom to live with?

It depends on their maturity level and what is best for them. I don't know. That's hard.

Boy, Age 10
Age at Time of Divorce: 10

1. How did you feel when your parents began to argue or when you began to notice that your parents were not happy?
I never really noticed.

2. How did your parents tell you what was going to happen?
They didn't.

3. How did you first feel about what was happening, when things started changing and your dad or mom stopped coming home or began coming home very late, or when one of your parents moved out?
Sad, kind of bothered.

4. What did your parents tell you about what was going to happen? How did they tell you?
We sat down, and Mom said she had filed a divorce against my dad and that things are going to be different.

5. What changes happened? Did you have to move, or did everything stay the same?
Dad moved out, and it was harder to get to places. One day you might miss your dad and you are at your mom's, then when you are at your dad's you miss your mom.

6. How did your parents change? How did they start acting around you?
They don't talk about each other as much as they used to. They wouldn't even mention each other.

7. How do you wish they would have handled the situation?
Better.

8. What was it like going to visit your dad or mom for the first time?

It was weird.

9. How do you feel about the times to visit? What is it like going back and forth? What if you forget something at the other house?

I don't like going back and forth. It was hard to get anything if you left it behind.

10. How has the divorce changed your life?

It's harder to live with this way.

11. How have your parents changed toward you? Are they acting different from when they were living in the same house?

Child did not answer.

12. What else can you tell me about how you feel?

Child did not answer.

13. What do you wish could be different?

That they wouldn't get divorced.

14. Do you think it's a good idea for kids twelve years old or older to have the power to choose whom to live with?

No, I wouldn't like to have that power.

Boy, Age 10
Age at Time of Divorce: 7

1. How did you feel when your parents began to argue or when you began to notice that your parents were not happy?

I didn't notice. I didn't hear them arguing because I was outside playing.

2. How did your parents tell you what was going to happen?

The police came to get Daddy out of the house. That's when I got concerned.

3. How did you first feel about what was happening, when things started changing and your dad or mom stopped coming home or began coming home very late, or when one of your parents moved out?

I felt concerned. I didn't know what was going on until then.

4. What did your parents tell you about what was going to happen? How did they tell you?

I found out. They didn't tell me.

5. What changes happened? Did you have to move, or did everything stay the same?

We had to move.

6. How did your parents change? How did they start acting around you?

They sort of changed. Mom talked more about what was going on.

7. How do you wish they would have handled the situation?

I didn't want them to get divorced. I wished they had stopped fighting, and I could have talked to them.

8. What was it like going to visit your dad or mom for the first time?

I don't remember. I do remember where he used to live.

9. How do you feel about the times to visit? What is it like going back and forth? What if you forget something at the other house?

It's boring. My sister said we couldn't call Mom unless we asked, and Dad always wants to know who I'm talking to. I didn't get it. Last Monday I had a choice as to whether I could go home at ten or only stay until six.

10. How has the divorce changed your life?
We don't live in the same house anymore. It's changed how I see my dad. A new marriage has changed my dad's life.

11. How have your parents changed toward you? Are they acting different from when they were living in the same house?
Mom doesn't act differently. Dad is whispering and talking about my mom behind me.

12. What else can you tell me about how you feel?
Child did not answer.

13. What do you wish could be different?
That they would stop fighting.

14. Do you think it's a good idea for kids twelve years old or older to have the power to choose whom to live with?
Not twelve, maybe fourteen. Not to move right then. Maybe to move when they're eighteen or nineteen.

Boy, Age 13
Age at Time of Divorce: 13

1. How did you feel when your parents began to argue or when you began to notice that your parents were not happy?
I had no clue.

2. How did your parents tell you what was going to happen?
They said, "Your mom and dad are having a hard time, so your dad won't be sleeping with your mom for a while."

3. How did you first feel about what was happening, when things started changing and your dad or mom stopped coming home or began coming home very late, or when one of your parents moved out?

Sad.

4. *What did your parents tell you about what was going to happen? How did they tell you?*

On a Monday all of us were at Grandpa's. I could tell Mom was edgy. She took all of us kids into the guest room, and she told us.

5. *What changes happened? Did you have to move, or did everything stay the same?*

Everything changed.

6. *How did your parents change? How did they start acting around you?*

Mom started changing the rules and Dad cried a lot.

7. *How do you wish they would have handled the situation?*

I wish they would have told all of us together. I was mad at my mom. She probably told lots of people. She said stuff that never happened like, "you can go over to your father's any time you want to."

8. *What was it like going to visit your dad or mom for the first time?*

I was quiet and sad and empty, physically, and I bet he was too.

9. *How do you feel about the times to visit? What is it like going back and forth? What if you forget something at the other house?*

Dad asked everyone to get Mom to get back together with him.

10. How has the divorce changed your life?

A lot. Dad took the computer to his house. I have two houses. For six years I wanted my own room. After the divorce, they made me a room.

11. How have your parents changed toward you? Are they acting different from when they were living in the same house?

Yes, we have all these different rules. I never heard these rules before.

12. What else can you tell me about how you feel?

Not good. Cheating is a good reason to get divorced. What really made me mad was that my mom asked to go along on my camp out and help, but when she found out my dad was going, she wouldn't go.

13. What do you wish could be different?

It would be nice if they got back together or if everyone would be happy.

14. Do you think it's a good idea for kids twelve years old or older to have the power to choose whom to live with?

Yes.

Girl, Age 11
Age at Time of Divorce: 4

1. How did you feel when your parents began to argue or when you began to notice that your parents were not happy?

I felt scared and upset. At nighttime they always made me go to bed early.

2. How did your parents tell you what was going to happen?

They told me at age four and a half. My sister was age three. They said it was like Dad was kind of going on vacation.

3. How did you first feel about what was happening, when things started changing and your dad or mom stopped coming home or began coming home very late, or when one of your parents moved out?

Mom had to work harder. We had to get a nanny and that made me upset because we didn't see Mom as much.

4. What did your parents tell you about what was going to happen? How did they tell you?

Mom told and said it wasn't her fault.

5. What changes happened? Did you have to move, or did everything stay the same?

Child did not answer.

6. How did your parents change? How did they start acting around you?

Mom didn't change. But I hardly saw my dad and didn't know why.

7. How do you wish they would have handled the situation?

I don't know.

8. What was it like going to visit your dad or mom for the first time?

It's okay, but it is different—it doesn't seem normal.

9. How do you feel about the times to visit? What is it like going back and forth? What if you forget something at the other house?

We can call.

10. How has the divorce changed your life?

Sort of.

11. How have your parents changed toward you? Are they acting different from when they were living in the same house?

Mom seems happier.

12. What else can you tell me about how you feel?

Child did not answer.

13. What do you wish could be different?

That my mom wouldn't have to work as much for money. She has to work on weekends, too.

14. Do you think it's a good idea for kids twelve years old or older to have the power to choose whom to live with?

I do.

Boy, Age 13
Age at Time of Divorce: 11

1. How did you feel when your parents began to argue or when you began to notice that your parents were not happy?

I was scared.

2. How did your parents tell you what was going to happen?

My mom just told me in the car that my father was going to leave and not stay.

3. How did you first feel about what was happening, when things started changing and your dad or mom stopped coming home or began coming home very late, or when one of your parents moved out?

They had separated once before, but they told me that everything was going to be okay. I was mad and really scared.

4. What did your parents tell you about what was going to happen? How did they tell you?

Mom told me most of the stuff and Dad told me some.

5. *What changes happened? Did you have to move, or did everything stay the same?*
Routines did change a little.

6. *How did your parents change? How did they start acting around you?*
Mom said, "You know your dad left us." My dad got a new dog. We used to all love our dog, now he makes fun of our dog.

7. *How do you wish they would have handled the situation?*
I wish they wouldn't have blamed everything on each other.

8. *What was it like going to visit your dad or mom for the first time?*
There were boxes everywhere and no room. I hated it.

9. *How do you feel about the times to visit? What is it like going back and forth? What if you forget something at the other house?*
My dad packs us up. If we forgot something he would go by and get it.

10. *How has the divorce changed your life?*
I don't see my father much anymore, and that makes me mad. It's different not having my father at home.

11. *How have your parents changed toward you? Are they acting different from when they were living in the same house?*
Mom hasn't changed. Dad is more generous, I think he wants me to like him more.

12. What else can you tell me about how you feel?

My dad used to make me do stuff. Now my mom doesn't make me do it.

13. What do you wish could be different?

I wish they would let us go through everything that was planned.

14. Do you think it's a good idea for kids twelve years old or older to have the power to choose whom to live with?

Yes. I think I should be able to choose. I would rather live in the house with my mom where I have lived my whole life than live in an apartment and go to a school I don't know anything about.

Girl, Age 12
Age at Time of Divorce: 2

1. How did you feel when your parents began to argue or when you began to notice that your parents were not happy?

I wasn't old enough to remember it now.

2. How did your parents tell you what was going to happen?

I don't remember.

3. How did you first feel about what was happening, when things started changing and your dad or mom stopped coming home or began coming home very late, or when one of your parents moved out?

Child did not answer.

4. What did your parents tell you about what was going to happen? How did they tell you?

5. What changes happened? Did you have to move, or did everything stay the same or did your routine change?

Child did not answer.

6. How did your parents change? How did they start acting around you?

Child did not answer.

7. How do you wish they would have handled the situation?

Child did not answer.

8. What was it like going to visit your dad or mom for the first time?

Child did not answer.

9. How do you feel about the times to visit? What is it like going back and forth? What if you forget something at the other house?

I got used to it. It's just like going over to a friend's house. If I forget something really important we'll go back and get it.

10. How has the divorce changed your life?

It seems like I have more to worry about. I have to worry about pleasing both parents. It's harder on a kid. There are more pressures than if they were married.

11. How have your parents changed toward you? Are they acting different from when they were living in the same house?

Child did not answer.

12. What else can you tell me about how you feel?

When they don't get along, it feels weird. I feel damned if I do and damned if I don't. The best divorce would be if rules and permissions were the same, and if they lived close together and you could be a week on and a week off with each parent.

13. What do you wish could be different?

To have more power. To have more freedom. Don't put pressure on kids. If they are ready to move they would. Don't worry about it. Don't talk bad about other people in other houses.

14. Do you think it's a good idea for kids twelve years old or older to have the power to choose whom to live with?
Child did not answer.

Girl, Age 12
Age at Time of Divorce: 6

1. How did you feel when your parents began to argue or when you began to notice that your parents were not happy?
I didn't notice.

2. How did your parents tell you what was going to happen?
They didn't really tell me.

3. How did you first feel about what was happening, when things started changing and your dad or mom stopped coming home or began coming home very late, or when one of your parents moved out?
I felt confused and I wondered why this was happening.

4. What did your parents tell you about what was going to happen? How did they tell you?
They said I was going to see my dad every other weekend and every Thursday. They said they want to live their own lives.

5. What changes happened? Did you have to move, or did everything stay the same?
Dad moved out, then we moved out, and Dad moved back in.

6. *How did your parents change? How did they start acting around you?*
Child did not answer.

7. *How do you wish they would have handled the situation?*
I wish they would have settled their problems without yelling.

8. *What was it like going to visit your dad or mom for the first time?*
I don't remember.

9. *How do you feel about the times to visit? What is it like going back and forth? What if you forget something at the other house?*
I started not wanting to spend the night because nothing goes on—we were just watching TV.

10. *How has the divorce changed your life?*
I don't have a real dad at my house now.

11. *How have your parents changed toward you? Are they acting different from when they were living in the same house?*

12. *What else can you tell me about how you feel?*
I don't like it.

13. *What do you wish could be different?*
I wish my parents would get back together.

14. *Do you think it's a good idea for kids twelve years old or older to have the power to choose whom to live with?*
I want to stay with my mom.

Girl, Age 10
Age at Time of Divorce: 6

1. How did you feel when your parents began to argue or when you began to notice that your parents were not happy?
I was only five or six at the time and didn't notice.

2. How did your parents tell you what was going to happen?
They didn't.

3. How did you first feel about what was happening, when things started changing and your dad or mom stopped coming home or began coming home very late, or when one of your parents moved out?
Dad left a three-page note and told Mom he had packed all of his stuff and would never come back. I saw my mom crying.

4. What did your parents tell you about what was going to happen? How did they tell you?
She read me the note and came out of her room crying.

5. What changes happened? Did you have to move, or did everything stay the same?
I had to have a baby-sitter. She worked for me for three years till she got married.

6. How did your parents change? How did they start acting around you?
I don't remember.

7. How do you wish they would have handled the situation?
I didn't know what they were fighting over. If it was bills or something, my mom could have gotten a job or should have worked hard to get a promotion.

8. What was it like going to visit your dad or mom for the first time?

It was a small apartment.

9. How do you feel about the times to visit? What is it like going back and forth? What if you forget something at the other house?

I got to visit my dad every weekend or every other weekend and spend the night. If I forgot something my mom would come over and give it to me, or my dad would bring it over.

10. How has the divorce changed your life?

It made it harder.

11. How have your parents changed toward you? Are they acting different from when they were living in the same house?

They're fighting more. I don't know who to believe.

12. What else can you tell me about how you feel?

I think soon there will be more divorces than marriages.

13. What do you wish could be different?

That my mom would get married to her boyfriend and my dad would find a girlfriend.

14. Do you think it's a good idea for kids twelve years old or older to have the power to choose whom to live with?

I wouldn't want it in a way. I wouldn't want to split me and my brother up.

Girl, Age 11
Age at Time of Divorce: 3

1. How did you feel when your parents began to argue or when you began to notice that your parents were not happy?

I couldn't tell. I was only three.

2. How did your parents tell you what was going to happen?

My dad came in and told me he was leaving. I made him sing three songs and kiss me sixty times.

3. How did you first feel about what was happening, when things started changing and your dad or mom stopped coming home or began coming home very late, or when one of your parents moved out?

I was sad.

4. What did your parents tell you about what was going to happen? How did they tell you?

I don't remember.

5. What changes happened? Did you have to move, or did everything stay the same?

My routine changed. At first I stayed in the same house and visited Dad at his place.

6. How did your parents change? How did they start acting around you?

They got in more arguments and seemed like they hated each other.

7. How do you wish they would have handled the situation?

By talking and not yelling.

8. What was it like going to visit your dad or mom for the first time?

Fun!

9. How do you feel about the times to visit? What is it like going back and forth? What if you forget something at the other house?

We go and get it, or my dad or mom gets mad at me.

10. How has the divorce changed your life?

My dad got married, and I got a little brother. My mom is getting married, and I'll have two brothers and two sisters.

11. How have your parents changed toward you? Are they acting different from when they were living in the same house?

Not really. My dad has always been more strict and Mom more easygoing.

12. What else can you tell me about how you feel?

Divorce is a hard thing for people to go through, but it turns out for the best because if parents can't get along, it's best for the kids.

13. What do you wish could be different?

Nothing.

14. Do you think it's a good idea for kids twelve years old or older to have the power to choose whom to live with?

Yes. Because if sometimes kids are living with one parent for a long time, they need an equal opportunity with the other parent.

Girl, Age 12
Age at Time of Divorce: 2

1. How did you feel when your parents began to argue or when you began to notice that your parents were not happy?

I was so young, I can't remember.

2. How did your parents tell you what was going to happen?

Child did not answer.

3. How did you first feel about what was happening, when things started changing and your dad or mom stopped coming home or began coming home very late, or when one of your parents moved out?

Child did not answer.

4. What did your parents tell you about what was going to happen? How did they tell you?

Child did not answer.

5. What changes happened? Did you have to move, or did everything stay the same?

My routine changed a lot. Every week I have a different parent.

6. How did your parents change? How did they start acting around you?

They are really nice as if it was a contest for my love.

7. How do you wish they would have handled the situation?

I wish they had seen a counselor.

8. What was it like going to visit your dad or mom for the first time?

Strange. I was suddenly more important than anything else.

9. How do you feel about the times to visit? What is it like going back and forth? What if you forget something at the other house?

The times to visit are always rough. Sometimes I slip up and call Dad "Mom" or Mom "Dad." If I forget something, I can call or go over to get it.

10. How has the divorce changed your life?

I think I could be a lot happier if they had stayed together.

11. How have your parents changed toward you? Are they acting different from when they were living in the same house?

Child did not answer.

12. What else can you tell me about how you feel?

I feel like a tug-of-war rope with my dad on one end and my mom on the other.

13. What do you wish could be different?

I wish my parents would back off and let me have room to breathe.

14. Do you think it's a good idea for kids twelve years old or older to have the power to choose whom to live with?

I think that when you are twelve to fourteen that you are mature enough to make your own decisions.

Boy, Age 8
Age at Time of Divorce: 8

1. How did you feel when your parents began to argue or when you began to notice that your parents were not happy?

I felt bad, and I wished that they would stop fighting.

2. How did your parents tell you what was going to happen?

They said to turn off the video games. Then they said, "We are getting a divorce." We said, "What's that?" Then they said, "We are getting separated." Then we cried.

3. How did you first feel about what was happening, when things started changing and your dad or mom stopped coming home or began coming home very late, or when one of your parents moved out?

I felt sad—like I wouldn't ever see my dad again.

4. What did your parents tell you about what was going to happen? How did they tell you?

Child did not answer.

5. What changes happened? Did you have to move, or did everything stay the same?

I kept the same nanny, but I had to go to bed earlier.

6. How did your parents change? How did they start acting around you?

At least they were not fighting at night.

7. How do you wish they would have handled the situation?

I wish they would have stopped fighting.

8. What was it like going to visit your dad or mom for the first time?

We went with him to pick out an apartment.

9. How do you feel about the times to visit? What is it like going back and forth? What if you forget something at the other house?

Child did not answer.

10. How has the divorce changed your life?

Child did not answer.

11. How have your parents changed toward you? Are they acting different from when they were living in the same house?

Child did not answer.

12. What else can you tell me about how you feel?

My dad already has a girlfriend. I think it was my mom's fault.

13. What do you wish could be different?

Child did not answer.

14. Do you think it's a good idea for kids twelve years old or older to have the power to choose whom to live with?

Child did not answer.

Boy, Age 13
Age at Time of Divorce: 10

1. How did you feel when your parents began to argue or when you began to notice that your parents were not happy?
I felt upset and worried.

2. How did your parents tell you what was going to happen?
We had a family meeting, and they just said they were going to get divorced.

3. How did you first feel about what was happening, when things started changing and your dad or mom stopped coming home or began coming home very late, or when one of your parents moved out?
I missed my dad when he left, and I didn't like my mom bringing home boyfriends.

4. What did your parents tell you about what was going to happen? How did they tell you?
Child did not answer.

5. What changes happened? Did you have to move, or did everything stay the same?
I had to move after a while.

6. How did your parents change? How did they start acting around you?
They didn't have as much time.

7. How do you wish they would have handled the situation?
They have handled it well.

8. What was it like going to visit your dad or mom for the first time?
Strange.

9. How do you feel about the times to visit? What is it like going back and forth? What if you forget something at the other house?

It's a pain going back and forth, but I like seeing each one. Forgetting something usually causes a pretty bad reaction.

10. How has the divorce changed your life?
A lot.

11. How have your parents changed toward you? Are they acting different from when they were living in the same house?
Not a whole lot.

12. What else can you tell me about how you feel?
Child did not answer.

13. What do you wish could be different?
Child did not answer.

14. Do you think it's a good idea for kids twelve years old or older to have the power to choose whom to live with?
Yes.

Man, age 23
Age at Time of Divorce: 5

1. How did you feel when your parents began to argue or when you began to notice that your parents were not happy?
I don't remember hearing anything.

2. How did your parents tell you what was going to happen?
My parents came into the bedroom and sat on the bed and said they had to tell us something serious—that they were going to separate. At the time, I thought that meant they would have separate bedrooms and closets.

3. How did you first feel about what was happening, when things started changing and your dad or mom stopped coming home or began coming home very late, or when one of your parents moved out?

I saw my grandpa moving Dad's stuff out of the house. Dad got an apartment three miles away.

4. What did your parents tell you about what was going to happen? How did they tell you?

My mom told me, "Your father and I don't love each other anymore."

5. What changes happened? Did you have to move, or did everything stay the same?

I would see my dad every weekend. It was kind of cool to go somewhere else. We did lots of things together and went to good places.

6. How did your parents change? How did they start acting around you?

Dad had more energy. Mom was very tired, determined, but tired.

7. How do you wish they would have handled the situation?

Child did not answer.

8. What was it like going to visit your dad or mom for the first time?

Sort of neat.

9. How do you feel about the times to visit? What is it like going back and forth? What if you forget something at the other house?

Child did not answer.

10. How has the divorce changed your life?

I missed my father a lot. It would get to me when I would see other families.

11. How have your parents changed toward you? Are they acting different from when they were living in the same house?
Child did not answer.

12. What else can you tell me about how you feel?
I have a bias that lots of things don't last forever.

13. What do you wish could be different?
Up to ninth or tenth grade, I wished they would have stayed together. Now I don't wish they had.

14. Do you think it's a good idea for kids twelve years old or older to have the power to choose whom to live with?
I don't know.

Boy, Age 11
Age at Time of Divorce: 3

1. How did you feel when your parents began to argue or when you began to notice that your parents were not happy?
I don't remember them getting mad at one another because I was too young.

2. How did your parents tell you what was going to happen?
Child did not answer.

3. How did you first feel about what was happening, when things started changing and your dad or mom stopped coming home or began coming home very late, or when one of your parents moved out?
Child did not answer.

4. What did your parents tell you about what was going to happen? How did they tell you?
I don't know.

5. What changes happened? Did you have to move, or did everything stay the same?
I don't know.

6. How did your parents change? How did they start acting around you?
Child did not answer.

7. How do you wish they would have handled the situation?
I was glad they got a divorce because if they hadn't, they would have five or six arguments a day.

8. What was it like going to visit your dad or mom for the first time?
They didn't argue in front of me.

9. How do you feel about the times to visit? What is it like going back and forth? What if you forget something at the other house?
Child did not answer.

10. How has the divorce changed your life?
I don't remember what it was like without a divorce.

11. How have your parents changed toward you? Are they acting different from when they were living in the same house?
Child did not answer.

12. What else can you tell me about how you feel?
Child did not answer.

13. What do you wish could be different?

That Mom and Dad would agree on more things like visits.

14. Do you think it's a good idea for kids twelve years old or older to have the power to choose whom to live with?
No, that's too scary. Too much pressure.

Girl, Age 10
Age at Time of Divorce: 7

1. How did you feel when your parents began to argue or when you began to notice that your parents were not happy?
Kind of sad.

2. How did your parents tell you what was going to happen?
They told me at the dinner table.

3. How did you first feel about what was happening, when things started changing and your dad or mom stopped coming home or began coming home very late, or when one of your parents moved out?
My dad went to live in an apartment.

4. What did your parents tell you about what was going to happen? How did they tell you?
They said they weren't happy with each other, and that they were going to separate for a while.

5. What changes happened? Did you have to move, or did everything stay the same?
We sold our house. After a couple of weeks, my brother moved out and went to live with my dad. My parents never said bad things about each other.

6. How did your parents change? How did they start acting around you?

It seems harder to talk to my dad. My mom has gotten more laid-back since her new husband is like that.

7. How do you wish they would have handled the situation?

I didn't understand it. I wish they would have explained it more. I wished they would have said they were getting a divorce instead of separating because I thought they would get back together.

8. What was it like going to visit your dad or mom for the first time?

It was weird. The apartment smelled weird. Dad was kind of shy. He didn't say a lot of stuff or be funny. He wasn't his regular self.

9. How do you feel about the times to visit? What is it like going back and forth? What if you forget something at the other house?

I'm afraid my Dad will say no, we can't go get it.

10. How has the divorce changed your life?

I feel kind of like ripped in two pieces. My mom tells me stuff and Dad tells me the opposite. I don't know who to believe, but I believe my mom.

11. How have your parents changed toward you? Are they acting different from when they were living in the same house?

12. What else can you tell me about how you feel?

It makes me sad because they don't like each other. My mom doesn't talk bad about my dad.

13. What do you wish could be different?

I wish my mom and dad had never met. I wish they could get along better.

14. Do you think it's a good idea for kids twelve years old or older to have the power to choose whom to live with?
Yes.

Girl, Age 11
Age at Time of Divorce: 9

1. How did you feel when your parents began to argue or when you began to notice that your parents were not happy?
It was a long time ago. I was about nine.

2. How did your parents tell you what was going to happen?
I heard my dad swing mom across the room. I hid and heard all the conversation. Mom started laughing, but Dad was crying. Usually though, women cry, men don't.

3. How did you first feel about what was happening, when things started changing and your dad or mom stopped coming home or began coming home very late, or when one of your parents moved out?
My mom got a job, and we started living at Grandma's house. Sometimes she slept with me.

4. What did your parents tell you about what was going to happen? How did they tell you?
They said, "We're not going to be living together." But I already knew.

5. What changes happened? Did you have to move, or did everything stay the same?
A lot stayed the same. We're still in the same house. Dad got custody. The judge just wanted money; he didn't care who he gave us to.

6. How did your parents change? How did they start acting around you?

They started being much nicer to each other.

7. How do you wish they would have handled the situation?

I wish they could agree on things. If you ask one, he tells you one thing, and the other tells you another thing.

8. What was it like going to visit your dad or mom for the first time?

I didn't mind it.

9. How do you feel about the times to visit? What is it like going back and forth? What if you forget something at the other house?

I feel like I don't have enough time with Mom. Time flies by. We always check before we leave to make sure I don't forget something.

10. How has the divorce changed your life?

My mom was always there. Every morning she would wake us up and give us breakfast. Dad didn't play a lot with us. Sometimes he would find time. My dad is doing all of this to impress the judges.

11. How have your parents changed toward you? Are they acting different from when they were living in the same house?

No.

12. What else can you tell me about how you feel?

Dad always got his way. Mom would give in. Mom always took care of us.

13. What do you wish could be different?

That I could live with my mom.

14. Do you think it's a good idea for kids twelve years old or older to have the power to choose whom to live with?

Child did not answer.

Boy, Age 13
Age at Time of Divorce: 9

1. How did you feel when your parents began to argue or when you began to notice that your parents were not happy?

I didn't listen to them, or I would go someplace else.

2. How did your parents tell you what was going to happen?

I don't remember how they did it, but I know my dad was gone for about a week or so.

3. How did you first feel about what was happening, when things started changing and your dad or mom stopped coming home or began coming home very late, or when one of your parents moved out?

Mom told me Dad was moving out.

4. What did your parents tell you about what was going to happen? How did they tell you?

They told me they were going to get separated. I didn't say anything. They told me I had to choose who to live with. At first I wanted to live with Mom, so Dad began bribing me.

5. What changes happened? Did you have to move, or did everything stay the same?

Child did not answer.

6. How did your parents change? How did they start acting around you?

Dad started being nice and going out and doing things with me. They never talked.

7. How do you wish they would have handled the situation?

I wish they wouldn't have done things with me everyday. I just wanted to stay home like normal people and act like nothing happened.

8. What was it like going to visit your dad or mom for the first time?

Like being home without my dad there. We were having fun like nothing happened.

9. How do you feel about the times to visit? What is it like going back and forth? What if you forget something at the other house?

At Mom's we never call my dad.

10. How has the divorce changed your life?

It hasn't made it better. It's supposed to be better, but everything is the worst.

11. How have your parents changed toward you? Are they acting different from when they were living in the same house?

Dad acts the same on the phone.

12. What else can you tell me about how you feel?

Child did not answer.

13. What do you wish could be different?

That everybody would get along. Then it would be okay.

14. Do you think it's a good idea for kids twelve years old or older to have the power to choose whom to live with?

Child did not answer.

Appendix II

Suggested Reading

For Kids

Dinosaurs Divorce, by Laurene and Marc Brown
Divorce Happens to the Nicest Kids, by Michael S. Prokop
The Duck's Divorce, by Steven J. Gross
I Think Divorce Stinks, by Marcia Lebowitz
My Mother's House, My Father's House, by C. Christiansen
The Not So Wicked Stepmother, by Lizi Boyd
What Am I Doing in a Stepfamily?, by Claire Berman
Why Are We Getting a Divorce?, by Florence Bienenfeld

For Parents

Divorce Book for Parents, Vicki Lansky
"The Divorce Page," a useful website on the Worldwide Web,
    maintained by Dean Hughson
Mom's House, Dad's House, by Isolina Ricca
*Second Chances: Men, Women and Children a Decade After
    Divorce,* by Judith S. Wallerstein and Sandra Blakeslee

Notes

Chapter 3

1. *Children and Families: Research and Practice,* pages 210–211.

Chapter 5

2. *The Dallas Morning News,* January 21, 1996, pages 1A, 22A, and 23A.

Chapter 6

3. Parenting Our Children: In the Best Interest of the Nation, A Report to the President and Congress, Submitted by the U.S. Commission on Child and Family Welfare, September 1996, page 3.

4. Parenting Our Children: In the Best Interest of the Nation, A Report to the President and Congress, Submitted by the U.S. Commission on Child and Family Welfare, September 1996, page 119.

5. *Child Custody Practice and Procedure,* chapter 4, pages 56 and 57.

6. Dividing the Child, page 116.

Chapter 7

7. Gardner, R. A. *The Parental Alienation Syndrome and the Differentiation Between Fabricated and Genuine Child Sex Abuse.* Cresskill, N.J.: Creative Therapeutics, 1987.

Chapter 8

8. Wallerstein, Judith S., Ph.D, and Blakeslee, Sandra, *Second Chances: Men, Women and Children a Decade After Divorce,* page 157.

Index